WILL WAY
PUBLISHING

West Long Branch, New Jersey

COPYRIGHT © 2024 MARIA L. PIANTANIDA, PMHNP-BC
Published by *Will Way Publishing*

ISBN   eBook   979-8-9905810-0-5
          Paperback 979-8-9905810-1-2

Library of Congress Control Number: 2024908630

First Edition
Book Production and Publishing by Brands Through Books
brandsthroughbooks.com

The

SIMPLE ART

of

GETTING

UNSTUCK

A Practical Guide to Unlocking Your Power

and Finding Fulfillment in Life

MARIA L. PIANTANIDA

PSYCHIATRIC MENTAL HEALTH NURSE PRACTITIONER

WILL WAY
PUBLISHING

To my husband, Dr. Paul Marquette, and my children Carter, Cassidy, and Cambrie, for their unwavering support not only for this book but for all my academic, professional, and athletic endeavors.

To my parents—Elaine Piantanida, for all the love a child could ever need, and my late father, Gary E. Piantanida, for teaching me what it means to never give up and instilling in me the confidence that I have the will to find the way.

To my cheerleaders—my brother Dan and my sister Lorraine—for their love and support, always, in everything I do.

PRIVACY STATEMENT

To respect the privacy of those friends and colleagues who may prefer not to be recognized and maintain client confidentiality, I have altered various personal details that might identify certain individuals and generally anonymized names.

DISCLAIMER

This publication contains the experience, research, opinions, and ideas of its author. It is intended to provide helpful and informative material on the subjects addressed. It is not a substitute for the medical recommendation of a physician or other healthcare provider.

This book is sold with the understanding that neither the author nor the publisher is engaged in rendering medical or other professional advice or services.

This book does not establish practitioner-patient relationship, and readers must consult their own physician or practitioner for the diagnosis, management, and treatment of their specific condition before adopting any of the suggestions in this book or drawing inferences from it.

The strategies outlined in this book may not be suitable for every individual. No warranty is made with respect to the accuracy or completeness of the information or references contained herein, and both the author and the publisher specifically disclaim any responsibility for any liability, loss or risk, personal or otherwise, which is incurred as a consequence, directly or indirectly, of the use and application of any of the contents of this book.

CONTENTS

INTRODUCTION

Welcome to *The Simple Art of Getting Unstuck: A Practical Guide to Unlocking Your Power and Finding Fulfillment in Life.*

Maybe you have anxiety or depression, or obsessive thoughts that you cannot get out of your head that cause worry and panic, creating the perfect storm for becoming stuck in unhappiness. Have you felt this way for so long that you cannot remember what it feels like to be happy? Are you irritable, snappish, or angry? I was. I was angry at myself, everyone in my life, and those I encountered who didn't understand why I was angry. It seemed I was angry at the world. Why? I didn't know. At first, I didn't even realize I was acting this way. I just knew I wasn't happy. Instead of kisses and hugs, I was sending my kids off to preschool every morning with irritability and impatience. Everything just seemed so much harder than it had to be. Every morning was a rush to get them out the door. Then I had to put a happy face on for others. It was exhausting. It didn't have to be that way. It shouldn't have been. I made it that way.

Do you feel like no one would understand or want to be around you if they knew what you were really like? Maybe you have no idea why you feel the way you do; you just know you don't want to feel this way any longer. Maybe it seems like you're stuck inside a hole that's too small to squeeze out of. You just can't fit through it, and you see no possible solutions for getting out. Or perhaps there are solutions, but you assume they can't possibly work for you because you're just too stuck. Maybe your sticking point is anxiety or depression. Maybe you engage in negative self-talk. Maybe you just can't get out of your own head or your own way. When you try, the voice inside your head may spin up doubt and uncertainty and tell you that you can't get out.

So, you quit trying, because that's easier and you don't believe you can get out anyway. This perpetuates a negative mindset that seems more impossible to break with each passing day. But it is not impossible, and you are not alone.

HERE'S WHAT THIS BOOK IS ABOUT

You can break the cycle of negativity. You can be happy. The process is not difficult, but you might need a little help. I feel your pain, trust me. I've got some real street cred with this. I've been there, and I can help.

You may be asking, why is the word *simple* in the title of this book? It's not because change itself is simple; it's because there's a simple, straightforward method that, once you apply it, can help you focus and direct your attention and get you to where you want to be. It's a science, but it's also an art. That's where the PAT method comes in. With it, you can create a custom process that fits your life and your needs. It takes thought and practice, but that's not hard. You can think, right? You can just as easily think about what's going well as what's going wrong. But it's easier to feel sorry that things are just not going well than to develop a plan to make them right. Believe me, I know the feeling. I was there. Instead of planning to solve my issues, I put on my sweatpants, old T-shirt, and fuzzy socks and stayed in bed. I bet you know what I'm talking about. It felt too overwhelming to think about how to get unstuck. Getting unstuck may seem like it's not within your power. But I'm here to tell you that not only is it within your power, it doesn't have to be complicated. How do I know? Because I was there and got unstuck.

WHAT IS THE PAT METHOD?

The PAT method involves tapping into the resiliency you already have that you strengthen by getting through tough times. It employs the use of simple but powerful techniques you can easily learn and do on your own to release yourself from the things that have been holding you down, preventing you from enjoying the life you deserve.

The first step in this process, P for past, will explain why it's important not to confuse your past situation with your current life. The past is the past, and it has little to do with the present.[1] Accept that things happened but leave them there. Instead of focusing on how badly you feel about past experiences, view them in terms of the knowledge you have gained and how you have learned to overcome them. Focus on your resiliency to overcome any future difficulties.

A is for attitude. Change your attitude to reflect acceptance of the things that have happened and gratitude for the strength to overcome them. Our attitude toward life and the struggles we've endured is what determines how we enjoy our lives. Share this gratitude in the form of kindness. When you show kindness, you notice kindness, and then kindness flows back to you. In this cycle, you'll notice a change in the way you view things in your world. The brain has the capacity to change after learning or experiencing something new. It is possible for you to change the way you think to more helpful patterns instead of ruminating on what's gone wrong. You can learn how to do this and develop helpful habits. This concept is called **neural plasticity,** and it will be explained in detail in later chapters.

T is for toolbox, which is an array of techniques and skills you'll learn in this book and can use whenever you need them to help you navigate tough times. These tools will be explained in detail in the coming chapters. Keep reading to see what they are and how they can help you.

WHO I AM AND WHY I WROTE THIS BOOK

I am a psychiatric nurse practitioner, and I have helped my patients get unstuck using my PAT method. This methodology was developed from years of experience and implementing the concepts into my own life. It explains how to get unstuck from the unhelpful habits and beliefs that have kept you stuck in a life you wish to change but don't know how to. I can help you discover how. I did it, my patients did it, and so can you. You can make a shift and enjoy the life you want and deserve. I want that for you. I want you to know what it feels like to get unstuck. Besides, your feet might stink from not changing your fuzzy socks.

Most people try to be positive but go about it the wrong way and give up because they want to see immediate results. But when your brain has been trained to think negatively for years, it takes some time to develop and strengthen different neural pathways to change the habit from negative to positive thinking. Scientific research shows that we as humans tend to focus more on the bad than the good.[2] We are more likely to pay attention to, learn from, and remember negative things than positive ones. This is what researchers Vaish, Grossman, and Woodward call the "negativity bias."[3] The authors further explain that this negative bias is evident as early as twelve months of age.[4]

Negative thinking is a pattern of thoughts that focuses on what's wrong or what could possibly go wrong. Negative thinking isn't helpful; it prevents us from developing solutions for what could work better because we're too focused on worrying about what might happen.

Maybe you don't think that you engage in negative thinking. I didn't think I did either. But we as humans tend to focus more on what we are not rather than on what we are. We don't make enough money, we have jobs that we feel stuck in, we're not as good at something as others are, we're not happy, etcetera. We focus on what isn't going well for us, what is uncomfortable, or what is overwhelming instead of on how to make it better. We tend to have expectations of what our lives should look like and then suffer from anxiety, anger, or sadness when reality doesn't meet those expectations. Focusing on what's going wrong keeps us in the wrong place. It creates a negative mindset that keeps us down. When we focus on the negative, we deprive our brains of positive experiences. When you want to do something well but you tell your brain that you don't think you can, then that's where your brain lives, in the negative zone of "I can't." It doesn't know you can because you tell it you can't. Or you leave it at "I'll try." But the brain doesn't know "try." It needs specifics: I can or I can't. If you tell it you can't, it will be really good at can't. Then, when you try to do whatever you want to do, your brain only knows "I can't" because that's what has been going on for a long time.⁵ It cannot help you. It has no positive experience to pull from. Want to change that? Tell yourself you can because you can.

WHO CAN THIS BOOK HELP?

So, here's the deal: you are not alone, and there is help. In this book, I will explain what symptoms are common in some of the disorders that cause people to feel stuck in their unhappiness. You may be experiencing symptoms that you don't realize are symptoms. You may not even be familiar with what a mental health symptom is. That's OK. I'll explain this later. I will help those who have not seen the benefit of traditional therapy learn how to manage or even eradicate their symptoms. I will identify those who may initially need more help than this book can provide and when they should seek professional help. I will not tell you what you must do, only what you can do. The choice is yours. I will drop the pearls. You must decide whether you pick them up. You are in control. But whatever you're experiencing and whatever your situation, I want you to know that you are not alone and there is help.

If you're feeling stuck where you are in your life, and you want to make changes to feel happier and experience a more fulfilling life but don't know where to begin, then this book is for you. Maybe you need professional help. Professional help looks different for everyone. It's possible you need therapy. Therapy can teach you the way to unlock your own ability to change your situation and your life. Maybe you need therapy and medication—because therapy takes time, and medication can start working sooner—so that you can focus on learning therapeutic techniques that can help you feel better.

Maybe you need more than therapy and medication. If you experience feelings of wanting to hurt yourself or someone else, please seek help at the nearest hospital emergency room so that you can be evaluated for the appropriate treatment. If you have experienced a mental health crisis or are going through one now and cannot get to the hospital, please do not hesitate to call 911, who will assist you in getting there safely. Some people are afraid to call 911 or of even going to the hospital because they fear they will be restrained or kept against their will. Please do not be afraid. The United States has laws to protect people from being held against their will. So do not let fear of the system impede the process of getting help. Get the help you need, and once you are stabilized, you will be discharged. The crisis staff will be eager to get you feeling better and back home to your loved ones.

If you experience visions that you're not certain are real, or if you hear voices that tell you to do or not do things, this is referred to as a hallucination, and it is also a mental health crisis. Hallucinations can be visual or auditory, and you will need acute care to relieve these symptoms. There are other types of hallucinations, but they are not common. Delusions are beliefs that are not based in reality, such as the belief that you have superpowers, are the president, or that you are receiving messages from the television or radio. These beliefs may feel very real at the time and even feel scary. If this is happening to you, please seek help at the nearest hospital emergency room.

Anyone experiencing what feels like bizarre behavior, such as risk-taking behavior, staying up for days at a time with no sleep and no need for sleep, or symptoms that severely impact their ability to function, should seek help at a hospital emergency room. These conditions are emergencies and require care in an acute setting such as a hospital. I urge you to take the step, seek help, and know that your crisis is temporary. After receiving some help to get stabilized, there is a community of professionals who can connect you with others who understand and can help you continue your journey toward wellness. Once you feel safe and stable again, please come back to this book. It will be waiting for you, and I invite you to read it.

You may be wondering, *what is a normal amount of sadness or anxiety, and how does this differ from symptoms of a condition that needs more help?* Good question. After all, we are human, and humans feel and express these emotions. We're allowed to be sad, be anxious, and worry about a problem, but we do not live in these emotions. We must return to our previous state of functioning and living after the incident causing them has been resolved. Prolonged grieving or worry is a problem. If you feel this may be happening to you, you should seek the advice of a professional.

When someone experiences sadness over the illness or death of a loved one, they grieve, and this process looks different for everyone. However, when grieving prevents one from returning to work or normal life, or interferes with activities of daily living, once the incident is over, this could be problematic. When emotions prevent us from enjoying the things we used to like to do or engaging with others due to fear or sadness, this is problematic. Help is available.

If you're unable to find happiness, or if you feel you're stuck in a miserable life, or if you're just getting through life but never fully enjoying anything, then this book is for you. My hope is that you will realize your purpose in the world. We all have one. Sometimes we just need a little help feeling better so that we can find it.

Maybe your past was difficult, and maybe it's holding you back from happiness because some unfortunate things happened that you cannot let go of. I'm in no way discounting or minimizing this or any pain you feel as a result. You cannot undo what has happened. But you can change how you react to it and what happens from now on. Your past is something that happened to you, not something that controls you. It does not define you as a person, and it will not continue happening unless you allow it to. As human beings, we learn from our experiences, both good and bad. If your past was not what you wanted it to be, don't dwell in it. Don't live in the past. Rewrite your story because you can. Change your path in life. Do what makes you happy. Feel you can't do it alone? There is help.

Everyone experiences emotional pain and suffering in different ways, and no one should ever tell you that you shouldn't feel the way you do or to just get over it. This is not a condemnation of how you have been dealing with your symptoms. I do not look down on anyone who does not agree with my methodology. It is a path to happiness but not the only path. And it does not imply that one can just think positively or take a deep breath and everything will be OK. No, it's simple, but not that simple. If it was, the universe would not need me, or any other mental health practitioners, and I would be looking for a new career. It is a process that takes some guidance, a little effort, a lot of patience, and time to create a new way of thinking and behaving.

This book is unique because it is a self-development/self-help book that goes a step further than most books to discuss issues that can interfere with enjoying a happy life from the perspective of someone who has both experienced these issues and treated those with symptoms. I also discuss medication and when one should consider it in addition to therapeutic behavioral interventions. I also provide information and guidance on where to find the right professional to address your needs, which can be so confusing.

This book will not discuss religion or religious beliefs. This book will provide basic information regarding medication, but it will not suggest that an individual should or should not take medications or what medications they should take. It is not an attempt to convince you to use any one method. Instead, it provides guidance for a place to start for anyone who is stuck where they are.

Some people are so stuck in their unhappiness and sadness that they cannot understand how to escape. The way out is right in front of them, they just can't see it. What is it? Everything. *Every. Little. Thing.* Things that make you feel good or bring you happiness. The blue sky, the beautiful flowers, your people, animals, nature, your home, your job, your health, etcetera—notice everything. When we stop for a minute to notice things that make us smile, we then notice other, bigger things, and it becomes something we just do. It becomes a habit: one that is helpful and that can change our lives for the better.

There are professionals like me who understand what you're going through. They get it, and they can provide therapy to teach you how to get unstuck. Think therapy takes too long? Medication can help so you can begin changing your story right now. Medication can allow you to feel better so that you can learn the techniques taught in therapy. You may not need to take medication forever. Once you learn how to move forward, you may be able to stop taking it. But you must be willing to try. Or, you can continue as you have been. That's an option. That's what I did for too long, and it didn't work. Don't do what I did. If you want to see a change, you must make one.

All of this and more will be discussed later in this book. And you'll be able to add these techniques to a toolbox for fixing what goes unexpectedly awry. You can use whatever is available to you to open your mind to the possibility of the power of a positive mindset. Many people have done it. Many of my patients did it, I did it, and so can you. My personal experience with postpartum depression, my more than thirty years of professional experience as a psychiatric nurse and then psychiatric nurse practitioner, and my education have provided me with insight into what causes people to get stuck. This insight was the impetus for me to research a way to help people get unstuck, and I decided to be part of the change I needed to see in the mental health system. I decided that the message must get out about how life-changing simple shifts in attitude, thinking, and behavior can be. I created the PAT method to help people just like you get unstuck from their unhappiness and learn how to enjoy their lives—because life is meant to be enjoyed.

YOU HAVE THE POWER—USE IT

You have the power to change your life, even if that feels impossible right now. Over the course of this book, we're going to explore where you might be stuck and how to refocus your mind on where you want to go. You can break the cycle of negativity. You can be happy, but you might need a little help. That's where I come in. You're stuck because of your view, your perspective, or what you believe. Life is hard. Shit happens. But these things don't need to control you or your life. We don't have to forget about these events, and we should process them. They happened. But they can make us stronger, smarter, and more powerful. There is another perspective of what happened to you or didn't happen for you.

We will discuss this concept of **cognitive restructuring** later, but right now, I will refer to it as changing the channel. Flip through your brain to a better channel—one that helps you move forward, out of the life you feel stuck in and into the life you want. This channel is one where you see the life you want. Enjoy that one instead of rewatching the one that keeps you limited to what you have been experiencing. Changing the channel is a decision. You can decide to feel better and enjoy what life has to offer you, or you can decide to stay stuck in a hole believing you just can't squeeze out. If you believe you're stuck, you will continue living in your stuckness. I think I made that word up, but you get my point. If you believe you have the power to get unstuck, then you're already on your way out of the hole.

When I implemented the techniques that became the PAT method, I noticed an immediate change in my life. I decided that my past was no longer relevant and had no place in my current life or future. Don't wait as long as I did to start enjoying your life. I am living proof that it works, and so are my patients. If I did it, and they did it, so can you.

Over the past few years, I've realized that my impact on my patients has been greater than I anticipated. Some have commented on my passion and energy in delivering my nontraditional therapy, and they have informed me that it has been life-changing, motivating, and empowering. Yet, I didn't do anything for them. I merely helped them open their minds to another form of therapy. What's different about what I do? It's a form of positive psychology, which is a type of psychology that points to the strengths and support people already have. It encourages the patient to focus on what's already good in life and uses this to remind them of their resiliency to help them move forward.[6] We will cover positive psychology more in chapter 4.

We can decide to stay stuck in our current situation, or we can make the choice to do what it takes to get unstuck and let go of the conflict that's keeping us down. We can choose to see the issues or the value in the conflict. There's something to be learned from every single thing, positive or negative, that happens in our lives. It's how we view these things that either causes us to be stuck or allows us to be free to live the lives we want. If we can see the benefit of an unfortunate incident, then we can work to make things better, to move forward. If you don't yet see the good that came from an event, wait for it, it will appear. We must realize that some things are for the universe to handle and the *why* is not so important. Focus on the process of moving forward and getting unstuck. Control what you can control, and release what you cannot. This might sound a little cold, but it's not. It might also sound a little like psychobabble, but trust me on this one. There will always come a time when we realize the benefit of something negative that happened. I'm not saying that it's a good thing that a loved one passed or that you experienced trauma. I'm just asking you to focus on what you can control now. I'm suggesting that you remember your loved ones and the joy that they brought you or what you gained from their presence in your life. I'm asking you to focus on the strength you gained from the extreme difficulties that you went through. The PAT method can be used to help you move forward from trauma after it's processed with a professional who is skilled in trauma therapy. You'll read more about this later.

In the following chapters, I hope to provide support and insight that will help you navigate the system of mental health and make sense of what you may be experiencing so that you can regain control of your brain and move forward toward a more enjoyable life. You can find happiness, and I want to save you some time and effort doing so. As the Stoic philosopher Marcus Aurelius put it, "Very little is needed to make a happy life; it is all within yourself, in your way of thinking."[7] If you're ready to discover more happiness in your own life, join me— just turn the page!

I Got Unstuck
and So Can You

"When you have exhausted all possibilities,
remember this: you haven't."[8]

—*Robert H. Schuller*

In this chapter, we'll address some of the ways you might feel stuck. Perhaps depression, anxiety, obsessive thinking, or perfectionism are robbing you of the enjoyment you could be experiencing in your life. We'll discuss what these conditions might look like and how to find help.

MY STORY (WELL, PART OF IT)

I was so depressed after the birth of my third child. I remember sitting on the floor in the playroom while cleaning up toys after putting my kids to bed and asking myself, *Why do I feel this way? I have three healthy children, a husband who loves us, a nice house, and a beautiful life. What is wrong with me?* My unhappiness bled into my relationship with my husband, and although he was a patient man, we divorced when the kids were older. I allowed my unhappiness to continue and to negatively impact my marriage. I couldn't enjoy my otherwise wonderful life. I focused on the problem and couldn't see a future free of sadness. I became so very angry at everyone and everything. I hurled my wedding dress down the attic stairs into the oil stains on the garage floor. My wedding album followed, falling into pieces.

As a nurse, I understood what was happening, but I didn't realize until I was in the thick of it that I was, in fact, suffering from depression. I demonstrated symptoms consistent with the criteria for diagnosing this condition according to the *Diagnostic and Statistical Manual of Mental Disorders,* fifth edition (DSM-5). This is a tool used by mental health professionals. It's a dense scientific text that includes standardized criteria for diagnosing mental disorders. I'll often refer to this book and break down the information it presents into more straightforward language.

The DSM-5 explains that depression is a feeling of sadness that becomes a problem when symptoms are out of proportion to a life event, such as an illness, the loss of a job, etcetera, and present for a specified period of time.[9] Sometimes, depression keeps us from doing the things we used to love to do, making us feel that we cannot find the energy to do them or no longer care if we do them or not. If these feelings are not the result of a temporary situation where they will subside once the circumstances are resolved, or they are accompanied by an inability to eat, sleep, or function in the usual manner or by symptoms of self-loathing, the inability to get out of bed to go to work or school, the inability to carry out daily activities, fatigue, guilt, weight gain or loss, hopelessness, suicidal thoughts, or self-harm and there is no medical explanation for the symptoms, professional help should be sought.

I thought my circumstances were beyond my control and that there was nothing I could do, so at first, I just dealt with them, which was really not dealing with them (medical professionals are such bad patients). To some extent, they were beyond my control. I had developed postpartum depression, and let me tell you, that shit is no joke! It's sadness mixed with hopelessness and topped with guilt, and let's not forget the daily fatigue that had me wanting to retreat to bed, where I could recover and not have to face the world. But I couldn't do that because I had a house to run, a family to care for, and responsibilities to maintain. And besides, recovery was temporary, because tomorrow was another day—another day to put on my happy face and carry on when I really felt like my head was a dumpster fire ready to explode.

Postpartum depression is depression that occurs after the delivery of a baby and involves hormonal changes. Fucking hormones. It is a very real condition that, if left untreated, can affect a woman's ability to care for her baby and herself. Although this was not my fault, my circumstances were mostly within my control. I could control how I viewed my past and my current situation and how I reacted to them. And I could have chosen to take medication to help me squeeze out of the deep hole I was in.

I finally made the decision to take medication, and it helped. But sometimes medication cannot solve the entire problem. The medication alleviated my postpartum depression, and I felt better, so I stopped taking it (again with the medical people). I was fine for a while, until I wasn't, and my symptoms returned. I'm not entirely sure if I was better or if I just got good at dealing with the symptoms. Maybe I adapted to my "new normal" without realizing what I was doing. Sometimes we go through life adjusting to our situation. Because that's what life is, right? Isn't it a series of adjustments to our experiences? Maybe—until we realize that this isn't how things should be. We continue to adapt until what's happening becomes our "normal." But is it? We just create our new normal because we're busy getting through life. And why? Why should we just get through it? That's not OK. That's not how life should be. But it was how life was for me for a while. I thought I was OK. Or maybe I convinced myself that I was. Looking back, I think it was the latter.

Despite what happened in my past, as a young adult, I had always been the eternal optimist. I adapted and thought that was, again, what everyone does. Everyone deals with these things, right? Others would say to me, "Maria, not everything is sunshine, rainbows, and butterflies."

When darkness descended like an eclipse on my life, my sunshine and rainbows were replaced by dark storms. My butterflies were gone. I began to feel overwhelmed with sadness and grief over the loss of my marriage and my family as I knew it. Fun seemed like a distant memory that I no longer deserved. I began to lash out at everyone for not being concerned enough and for abandoning me, and I looked for their ulterior motives when they did show concern. They couldn't win. I was miserable. Things were bad. When they would ask me to try to be more positive, my response was "Positive?! Fuck your positivity! Do you not see my life right now?" But they couldn't see why I was this way. They saw a different life than what I was seeing. I was divorced from reality as well as from my husband. I was not fun to be around, and so no one wanted to be around me. I felt so alone. But I wasn't alone. I just chose to believe that I was. It was an opinion, a negative bias.

Depression, the soul-sucking monster, continued to worsen, fighting me with the stealth of a ninja warrior. Before I knew it, I became someone even I didn't like. In reality, it was me—I was causing the problem. I created scenarios that confirmed and perpetuated my flawed belief that I wasn't worthy or that others didn't care. I began ruminating about my past hardships and pain. I rejected any help offered by others with my angry behavior. I resented everyone for not noticing my pain. The resentment kept me down, angry, and irritable. It limited me in everything I did. I felt small, fragile, and helpless. I couldn't notice the beauty that was right in front of me. The same beautiful things that made me stop and smile became the mud puddle that I stepped in and cursed.

My depression worsened over time, and my self-esteem was

worse than ever. I started to think about my past and blame my parents and the trauma I went through during my childhood for my unhappiness. That's how it is, right? Someone or something is to blame for this situation. I was stuck. I was angry about what happened to me, so my mission was to let everyone know it. I was so wrong. Things did happen to me through no fault of my own, but I was responsible for my reaction to past events. I was too focused on what was wrong in my life to see what was right in front of me, the beauty of my life. I was too focused on the negative to see the possibility of a bright future. I was so focused on wallowing in my sadness that I didn't reach out. I thought those I loved should know I was upset and needed help. But people do not have the ability to read minds, which is essentially what I was expecting of them.

DIAGNOSIS—WHAT IS IT AND WHY IS IT NECESSARY?

Symptoms of anxiety, depression, ADHD, and obsessive thinking look different for everyone, but there are some common symptoms that lead to a diagnosis. Being diagnosed with a disorder is not a bad thing. Really, it isn't. Don't flip out. Be thankful that you know why you feel the way you do and that there's help to get through it. A diagnosis is necessary because it provides guidance for treatment. If you have X symptoms, you may benefit from Y treatment or Z medication. Diagnoses provide a starting point for treatment so that your valuable time, time that could be spent feeling better, is not wasted trying treatments for a disorder you may not have.

We covered depression in the previous section, and now we will address other conditions that cause people to feel stuck. Please know that symptoms cross over, which means that some symptoms are common in more than one disorder, and it is important to evaluate all symptoms to see what condition best explains the symptoms or to see if there are co-occurring conditions that require simultaneous treatments. Luckily, there are medications that can treat multiple conditions. This will be addressed later.

ANXIETY

Anxiety sucks. It's a feeling that something is wrong but you can't figure out what, or you know what it is and worry about it too much. Feelings of impending doom are common with anxiety and very scary. Impending doom is the sense that something big is about to go wrong, but you don't know what. Maybe you feel that if you don't worry about something, it may happen. So, you relieve the anxiety by thinking of every scenario that could happen. Anxiety may prevent you from doing things out of fear that something bad will happen. It may be associated with some physical symptoms such as increased heart or respiratory rate, chest discomfort, restlessness, irritability, difficulty concentrating, difficulty eating or sleeping, muscle tension, headache, stomachache, or fatigue.

When the worry is out of proportion to a normal life event and does not subside when the event is over, like anxiety about a test, a performance, or a medical procedure, it may be excessive. If anxiety happens too often, does not subside, has no apparent cause, is difficult to control, or significantly interferes with normal activities of daily living, this is a sign that you need to seek professional help. Help is a phone call away.

People with anxiety often worry about their health or the health of their loved ones when there's no medical issue going on, or in spite of a logical explanation for something minor that happened. Sometimes, a logical explanation for a rash, a strange feeling, a "skipped heartbeat," or other minor issue does not satisfy an anxious person who worries that it could be something worse. Sometimes, anxiety can be very debilitating and lead to depression. If anxiety interferes with your ability to get normal daily activities done, or causes significant distress, you could have a problem that needs professional help.

For me, it felt like everything went wrong. Everything was so much harder than it should have been. In addition to feeling sad, this caused me a considerable amount of anxiety. I couldn't get things done, and I worried about everything I still had to do. I wanted my beautiful outlook on life back. I wanted my rainbows and butterflies. I wanted to feel happy and productive. So, I decided to do something different. I decided that I didn't have to accept things as they were. I was tired of feeling sad and struggling with everything I had to do. I got serious. I dug deep and wrote down everything that was good in my life that I pushed down and ignored. I read it over and over. I realized that I wasn't alone and had people who loved me. I became grateful for what and who I had in my life. I viewed my past as something that happened to me but not something that could control me. It was not happening anymore, but I was keeping it alive. I didn't have to do that. I didn't have to be what I didn't want to be. I could be different, and so I decided to be. I rewrote my story. This was my first step in developing the PAT method, but I didn't even realize it yet.

What I was doing for so long was not helping, and since you are reading this book, I'm guessing that what you're doing isn't working either. I learned how to change my perspective and see my life differently. I opened my mind and started to appreciate what and who I had in my life, what was right in front of me. I decided to focus on what was good and how I could change what was not instead of wallowing in what was wrong. I wanted to be happier, so I decided to be happier, and you can too. I want that for you and for everyone who is suffering needlessly, because it does not have to be that way. In the words of Abe Lincoln, "Folks are usually about as happy as they make up their minds to be."[10] Make up your mind that you *can* be happy and ask for help. Do it now. Help is available.

OBSESSIVE-COMPULSIVE DISORDER (OCD)

Obsessive thoughts get stuck, causing us to feel stuck.

Obsessive thoughts are those that cannot be stopped and continue despite attempts to think of something else. If the thoughts happen most days, many times a day, and interfere with school, work, social activities, or relationships, professional help should be sought. Common obsessive thoughts, as explained in the DSM-5, are those that revolve around health, cleanliness, fears of germs, fears of saying or not saying the right things and being embarrassed, fears of doing horrible things that you would never actually do, hurting people or their feelings, or sexual inappropriateness.[11] Some people suffer in silence with these thoughts, as they feel guilty or freakish for having them. This could not be further from the truth. Everyone has experienced bizarre thoughts at some time. Everyone! These thoughts become problematic for some people when they listen to them and worry about them until they get stuck. The brain is a complex organ, and sometimes it seems to work against us. But that can be changed. You can change it and get unstuck.

When these thoughts happen and you give them credibility and begin to listen to them, they can get stuck. They can cause anxiety and apprehensive anxiety, which is worry about if and when the anxiety or the thought will come. This is essentially worry about worry. It's worrying even during the times you're not experiencing anxious thoughts, therefore causing you to spend more time worrying than not worrying. The more we worry about the anxious thoughts coming, the more they come, and then they get stuck, and it seems like we can't think of anything without them popping in like an idea. But this idea isn't motivating. It's like a bad dream in the time loop from *Groundhog Day* (you know the movie), except this bad dream isn't funny at all.

Everyone has bizarre thoughts at times. But thoughts cannot hurt us. It's helpful to ignore them and to tell your brain that they are simply thoughts. But when your brain is a war zone of those battling thoughts fighting it out, causing your head to feel like it will explode at any minute, that's kind of difficult, right? If you could ignore them, you would have done that by now, right? You can learn how to do this. It is possible to stop the war and call a truce with obsessive thoughts. But we cannot rationalize them away. Winston and Seif, in their book *Overcoming Unwanted Intrusive Thoughts*, explain that rationalizing doesn't work because it gives attention to the thoughts, causing them to stick around.[12] It takes some time to rid yourself of these worries, and if necessary, medication can help until you learn the coping skills in therapy to recognize and reduce the thoughts and eventually extinguish them.

Perfectionism is a type of obsessive thinking that robs us of our ability to enjoy life. It feels like nothing is ever "right" enough for us. We obsess about how we can be better, and we are not able to experience the satisfaction of doing something good. The constant focus on being better prevents us from enjoying what we've done. We get stuck in a pattern of redoing everything, and it becomes time-consuming, negatively impacting productivity and success. Dr. Maxwell Maltz has done quite a bit of research on why people do this. He cautions his readers that good must be enough sometimes.[13] Better is not always possible, and striving for this not only deprives us of experiencing joy but increases our stress, adding to physical and mental symptoms. We must allow our brains to feel and experience satisfaction, success, and productivity if we want to be satisfied, successful, and productive people.

Even worse is when we compare what we do, what we are, or what we feel we are to others, trying to be a version of perfect that we believe others are. When this isn't achievable, we suffer from a comparison that isn't really there and that only exists in our own minds. We see only a snapshot of what we think is a reality that we want. When it cannot become reality, we suffer disappointment and, sometimes, depression. Why do we do this? Why not instead practice "good enough?" Social media has increased the severity and occurrence of these issues, and many people, especially young people, spend too much time comparing themselves to snapshots of the lives of others on social media. They are fooled by the happy moment in the post and become dissatisfied with their own lives because they think they should be more like the people they're viewing. This leads to decreased self-esteem, depression, and sometimes even worse.

Remember the concept of neural plasticity introduced earlier? This is the brain's capacity to change after learning something new. Neural pathways are strengthened whether the information is negative or positive. Perfectionism reinforces the negative, unhelpful pathways. It provides the brain with negative experiences to recall instead of positive ones. This is not productive. Allow your brain to feel that something is good enough. As Dr. Maltz points out, allowing good to be enough "takes off the strain, relaxes you, [and] enables you to perform better."[14] Help your brain recall past successes, not failures. Remind yourself how good those past successes felt so your brain can use this image and feeling to form what I refer to as **power pathways** to perform better, instead of negative, unhelpful pathways that keep you down. We'll talk more about these pathways later.

You'll see that I refer to Dr. Maxwell Maltz quite a bit in this book. He was a plastic surgeon turned psychologist and author after discovering that some of his patients didn't feel happier after their facial deformities were corrected by his surgical interventions. Although most felt they had changed for the better, some felt that their scars were too deep emotionally for them to ever feel healed and happier. He decided that he could help more people by becoming a psychologist. His research and book provided inspiration for me in my practice. I wish I'd had the opportunity to meet this amazing man before he passed.

COMPULSION—THE MUST-DO PART OF OCD

Some people suffer from compulsive acts that they worry about over and over, such as checking doors to be sure they're locked or appliances to be sure they're turned off. They feel stress or anxiety until they check, and sometimes must check again, even if they know they've already checked them. Some people take pictures with their phones to prove they performed the act but still doubt they did. Some people check and recheck, but this does not interfere with their life in any way. Others obsess about these things and check over and over, preventing them from getting their work or other things done, causing a significant negative impact on their life. Some people feel ashamed that they cannot get things done, are repeatedly late for work or social events, or affect their loved ones by their constant need to check. They feel stuck in this pattern of behavior and don't know how to stop. If this sounds like you, you may benefit from exposure and response prevention therapy, which is a therapeutic technique that, over time, decreases and eventually extinguishes the compulsive act. Medication can help until therapeutic behavioral techniques can be learned in therapy.

This leads me to another common disorder that people often feel ashamed or guilty about experiencing. And talk about feeling stuck, some people are literally unable to do things as a result of the next condition.

ATTENTION DEFICIT HYPERACTIVITY DISORDER (ADHD)

ADHD is another very common problem that causes people to feel stuck. Sometimes, people don't even know that they have it. They just know that things are more difficult for them than for others. They often become exhausted from the things they must do to try and keep up with their lives. This disorder is characterized by an inability to focus, maintain concentration, remember, organize tasks, or get things done. It can be extremely frustrating and interfere with one's ability to succeed at work or in school. It may lead to poor grades or loss of employment because things are just not getting done. For example, I treat an attorney who lost his job while we were attempting to find the right medication at the best dose for him. I wish he had come to me sooner—and no doubt, so does he—but his symptoms of procrastination, lack of motivation, and disorganization got in the way of seeking help.

This condition can seriously impact one's ability to feel good about themself and can lead to avoidance of certain experiences for fear of failure. It can also be associated with an inability to rest or enjoy relaxing activities. If symptoms interfere with work, school, or forming or keeping social relationships, professional help should be sought for medication management, as this condition most often requires both medication and therapy to learn behavioral techniques to manage symptoms. Medication cannot cure the condition, but it can greatly increase success, self-esteem, and productivity by helping the brain remain focused by modulating the number of neurotransmitters responsible for these functions. Medications to treat ADHD essentially help the brain get unstuck so it can become more focused, attentive, and productive.

WHAT HELP LOOKS LIKE

Some symptoms can be effectively treated with therapy—often referred to as talk therapy. Who can do this and how do you find them? You can ask your primary care doctor for recommendations. They often receive referrals from therapists who think their clients could benefit from medication, and so the referral base goes both ways. A good place to search online is Psychology Today, which is a database of therapists, where they are located, and what areas they specialize in, with brief bios on everyone. Another good idea is to ask others who you know are engaging in therapy. If they're happy with their therapist, get a contact number and call them. Since insurance companies dictate so much of medical and mental health care, calling your customer service number to ask who's in your network and what benefits you have can also be beneficial.

Therapists are trained mental health professionals who can help make sense of feelings that keep you from doing what you want or love to do. They can help you process events in your past that may be contributing to your current problem. They can help you discover why you feel the way you do and provide insight into your symptoms. Therapists are very good at helping you to realize what you need to do to move forward. They can diagnose certain mental health conditions and refer you to someone who can prescribe you medications. Most therapists take insurance, but not all of them do, so remember to ask.

Nurse practitioners can diagnose conditions, prescribe medications, and provide therapy. However, most mental health nurse practitioners prefer to just prescribe medication, as that's the focus of their training. They are all trained to provide therapy, but this part of their training is not as comprehensive as that of a therapist, who spends their entire education and thousands of hours on therapy alone. Most nurse practitioners accept insurance. In fact, the reason nurse practitioners are so popular is that they fill the gap in care for people who cannot pay out of pocket for their mental health care when their psychiatrist or other practitioner does not accept their insurance.

Physician assistants can also diagnose conditions, prescribe medication, and provide therapy. They are very similar to nurse practitioners in clinical practice, but their training is a little different. However, the difference is more behind the scenes, and patients will not notice any difference in clinical practice.

Psychiatrists can diagnose conditions, prescribe medication, and provide therapy. However, only some psychiatrists in private practice provide therapy, and it's becoming less common for them to do so. If therapy is what you need, it's important to determine if they offer it before scheduling an appointment. It's also important to determine if they accept insurance since it's becoming less common for psychiatrists to participate in insurance plans, and paying out of pocket can be cost-prohibitive for many people.

Mental health coaches and life coaches cannot diagnose, provide therapy, or prescribe medication, but they can help you make behavioral changes to get you where you want to be on your mental health journey. They complement therapists, nurse practitioners, and psychiatrists in teaching you how to recognize issues and becoming more motivated to make changes and create better habits.

WHY THIS BOOK AND MY BACKGROUND CAN HELP

In this book, I intend to share what I've learned through my personal experience, education, and over thirty years of professional practice, first as a psychiatric nurse and then as a mental health nurse practitioner, treating people just like you. I've worked in many different mental health settings with children, teenagers, and adults. I have extensive knowledge of the pain, suffering, and devastation mental illness can cause individuals and their families.

I started working in mental health in a community hospital on a voluntary inpatient unit, and then moved to a locked, acute care setting at a major university hospital in Center City, Philadelphia. That was an experience! I quickly learned about the revolving door of the mental health system. It saddened me to see individuals enter the hospital, get better, and leave the hospital, only to return a few months or a year later with the same problems.

I then worked in a group home setting for children and teens for six years. This was a residential program that provided intense psychiatric care to mostly children and adolescents while they lived away from their families in a group home, for at least a year but often longer. This was a revolving door as well.

After that, I took a part-time job at an assisted living facility, where I provided medical and mental health care for elderly individuals at the end of their lives. This is a place where elderly people reside when they cannot live independently due to difficulties associated with aging. I also worked at an adult respite center for drug- and alcohol-addicted individuals with mental health disorders who had lost their housing, had nowhere to go, and needed treatment. Another revolving door.

I became a nurse practitioner to increase access for those who couldn't get care because either their provider didn't take insurance or they lost their insurance when they changed or lost their job. For whatever reason, they needed someone who was competent, understood their struggle, and cared enough to give a shit about their situation and their future well-being. That was me. I wanted the system to change. I wanted to help, and I want to help you too. My PAT method can show you how to change your life so that you can create your own happiness and live the life you want to. You deserve to be happy, and you can be.

One of the biggest differences between happy people and unhappy people is what they choose to focus their attention on. Happy people get sad too. They just decide not to live in that emotion for very long. They allow themselves to feel the sadness but then move on to see how they can change things to feel better. Their focus is on happiness. They view their problems as something to solve, not to live with or dwell on. They leave the past behind and recognize that it doesn't have to dictate what they feel in the present. Unhappy people tend to focus all their attention on their problems and live in that headspace. They constantly think of their situation, why it happened, and how bad it is instead of on ways to improve it. They might take steps to correct it, but their focus remains on the negative. I'm not pointing fingers. I'm guilty as charged for doing this, but I found out how to stop. I acknowledged my past issues because, let's face it, they happened, but I realized that they weren't still happening and that my life was different. I stopped reliving them in my mind. You can stop too. I used the PAT method to leave the past in the past. That single decision helped shift my attitude.

I am living proof that this technique works, and that it works well. I'm an optimist, but I was not a believer in creating my own happiness. I thought that was psychobabble. I opened my mind when I realized that I was focusing on my past and what happened to me more than on what made me happy. I was limiting myself to sadness and blocking happiness from entering my life like a boxer blocking blows. I was giving sadness too much of my time and energy, and the negative thoughts too much power. I allowed them to take control and dictate my actions. I noticed that I didn't feel good when I was stuck in this thought pattern. What I was doing wasn't helping me. It wasn't working for me. I was tired of feeling like I was just going through the motions of life. That was no way to live. I realized that there are so many things that I enjoy that make me feel good. Why was I not doing them, enjoying them? I made the decision to focus on what was good in my life. The moment I decided to do this, I noticed things were easier and that more good things were happening. My attitude shifted from *Things happened to me that I cannot change* to *What can I change to become happier?* I started noticing things that made me feel good instead of focusing on what made me feel bad. I intended to learn more about this.

I began to read everything available on this topic and to then tell others what I learned. I let go of resentment and my perspective on what happened to me. I stopped blaming others and changed my attitude. I decided to pay it forward. This was the moment when things really started to get better for me, when I decided to turn my knowledge into power—power that could help me but also help others. That became my mission. I hope to provide insight that will help you navigate the system of mental health and make sense of what you may be experiencing so that you can regain control of your brain and move forward toward a more enjoyable life. I hope to help you see that holding onto your past and being stuck in your frustration, anxiety, sadness, obsessive or intrusive thoughts, lack of focus, lack of direction, and negativity prevents you from living a meaningful, enjoyable life. I hope to save you time figuring out how to get unstuck. You can find joy and meaning in life. You can improve your self-esteem and confidence by shifting your attitude. You can enjoy the people you love instead of missing out on time with them by employing the tools you will learn in this book and by using the PAT method. You *can* be happy! Keep reading to learn how.

Be kind to yourself—the universe needs you.

CHAPTER 2

THE PAST IS THE PAST.
LET GO OF THAT SHIT!

"You can't go back and make a new start, but you can
start right now and make a brand new ending."[15]

—*James R. Sherman*

The first step in the PAT method is to separate your past from your
current life and not confuse the two. The past is over. It does not
have to control who you are or how you behave now unless you allow
it to. The above quote by James R. Sherman explains that negative
things happen, but it is our reaction to them, our perception of them,
and our judgment of how bad they are that truly makes them problematic. In his book *Psycho-Cybernetics*, Dr. Maxwell Maltz explains
that these are all just opinions, not facts, and that we can choose to
believe or not believe them.[16] Something can be truly horrible, but
this is our opinion of the event. It might not be horrible for someone
else. Check your opinions on mistakes you've made in the past. Make
sure you're not judging yourself or others too harshly. Be kind to the
current version of yourself, who is moving forward with grace and
compassion. You deserve to feel great. You are here for a reason, even
if you do not yet know what it is.

Allow yourself to discover all that awaits you. You are not what
happened to you. You are not your past. Your past has no control over
you and cannot dictate who you will be in the future. You have the
power to control how you feel, what you do, and how you do it. No

one else has that power over you. You may believe that this is not simple, but it is as simple as deciding to do it. In the words of Dr. Maxwell Maltz, "If you can remember, worry, or tie your shoe, you can succeed."[17] What he meant by this is if you can do things that any human being can do and does repeatedly, regardless of education or experience, then you can succeed at changing your life. You can be happy if you want to. But you must make the decision to do so, and you must believe that you can. I can show you how. In fact, I'm excited to show you how simple it can be.

GET OUT OF YOUR OWN WAY

Life is hard and bad things happen to good people, but it is how we view what happened that's important. It's OK to feel sad about not getting a promotion that you thought you would get, for losing your job or about a breakup, and of course, it's normal to feel sad when someone passes away. These are human emotions that all people feel at times, and no one should feel guilty for feeling that way. But anger, frustration, and sadness are temporary, and we can move forward and remember that our life has purpose and is worth living happily, regardless of what has happened.

We don't have to forget what happened, but we can learn to experience sadness as a normal human emotion, remembering that there is goodness after an unfortunate event. Every single thing that happens has another perspective waiting to be realized. We may not figure out what that is until years after the experience, but it will definitely become apparent. These negative events may be a necessary step toward something different or better waiting for us in the future. We may be led down a path that we may never have taken if not for the unfortunate event. You have a choice: you can focus on what happened and why it's bad, or you can change your view and find a way to grow from it. Continue wallowing or change the channel, you decide. You have control. As Napoleon Hill once said, "Every adversity, every failure, every heartbreak, carries with it the seed of an equal or greater benefit."[18]

This changing the channel is cognitive restructuring, a technique used to help people understand that they may not be seeing the whole picture and that things may not be as bad as they believe them to be. Sometimes we focus on our opinion of a situation and lose sight of the reality that another view exists. I understand that this may sound like psychobabble. A good side to something bad? WTF? But stick with me on this and you won't be sorry. It'll make sense, I promise.

You can start immediately and experience happiness by focusing your energy and attention on what's going well in your life right now. What have you got to lose? Start to notice everything that makes you happy, brings you joy, or causes you to smile. Do yourself a huge favor: choose to stop focusing on what's wrong and why, which limits you in what you can achieve in life. It keeps you in your own way. Get out of your way. You can even think about things in the past that have gone well for you or that have made you happy. Dr. Maltz assures us that it doesn't matter what this memory is or how significant it is. As long as it's a good, happy one, it can help you.[19] Remember, your brain can help or hurt you. Allow it to help you by forming power pathways. Allow it to turn these positive thoughts into memories that can be recalled when you need them. Don't miss the opportunity to do this whenever something good happens that makes you feel happy or proud. Start by using the PAT method to cultivate happiness, get unstuck, and break the ties to past unhappiness.

I learned how to prevent my past traumatic events from affecting my adult life by using the PAT method. The events of my past happened, but they're not still happening. I don't allow them to occupy space in my brain. I view them in terms of how strong I am after overcoming them. I also learned to see the other side—the silver lining. Yes, even in a horrible situation, I was able to find the upside. If you had asked me to do that years ago, I would have told you to fuck off. But today, I appreciate the outcome of past events, such as how my once difficult relationship with my father later became a positive one that helped me grow and become the strong woman I am today. I learned how to separate past events from my current life. I wish I had figured out how to do this sooner, but regardless, I am grateful.

WEATHERING THE STORMS

I grew up in a tumultuous household with an angry father, which caused a great deal of problems for me and my family. He was very protective and loved his family but was trying so hard to provide for us that he lost himself. He made living with him very difficult, and we were afraid of him most of the time. He became a victim of his own anger and self-loathing because he felt like he failed to provide for us, and we fell victim to his anger and hostility. This, coupled with a horrible childhood spent trying to earn the praise of a father who was impossible to please and would never be proud of him, was a recipe for disaster for everyone involved. He allowed his past to define him and took his frustrations out on his family for so long. He was stuck.

Finally, he realized that his father's approval was neither coming nor worth anything. That's when he recognized he was something more than who his father told him he was. He didn't have to be like his father. He didn't have to perpetuate the negative cycle. He learned this late in life, but he always told me I could do whatever I wanted and to never let anyone tell me I couldn't do something. He was trying to prevent me from being like him and was not even aware of it. He was trying to leave his past in the past. I should have listened more intently.

My mother complemented him very well, but it took a toll on her as well. She was and still is the kindest woman to ever live. She put up with him and his anger at himself, which he took out on us. This was what he had learned. He knew nothing else. He had no positive role model. But somehow, he learned to change. With the help of my mother, who provided unwavering love and support, he learned to rewrite his story. She spread kindness wherever she went. Despite her negative environment, she was nothing but kind. She was grateful for what little she had. She noticed everything wonderful in life and made a point of showing others. She noticed the small things. She stopped and smelled the roses whenever she could. She epitomized positivity even when things got dark, and they got really dark. Storms happened. Out of blue skies, thunder and lightning descended on our house like a bad hurricane. Domestic violence is a nightmare that feels unending and impossible to fix, especially when you're a child.

This is another one of the occasions where I "adjusted" to my situation. I became accustomed to acting in ways that would not make my father angry. We all did this to mitigate the damage that would inevitably happen when he was anxious or angry, or dealing with a problem, which usually involved finances. He never used drugs or alcohol. Anger was his problem. One night, there was no amount of adjusting that would help prevent an incident. I had to call the police on my father. I remember thinking, *WHAT? Is this really fucking happening? Am I really doing this?*

It was and I was. Something different had to be done to break the cycle. After this, my dad was prevented from entering the house by a restraining order. He was ordered by the courts to get help. He knew he had to, or he would lose everything that meant anything to him. We were all he had. He got help. Things got better, but he was still angry and unhappy.

My father was a victim of his past. I was a victim of my father's anger. But I decided I would not let my past define me. I decided to leave that in the past and focus on my resiliency. I am no longer a victim. However, I waited longer than I should have to realize this. Things did happen, and I became stuck. I hope to save you some time, energy, and heartache by teaching you how to get unstuck now.

THE SLIPPERY SLOPE

Over the past thirty years working as a nurse and then a nurse practitioner, I've realized that no matter how much therapy some people receive, or how much time they devote to working on getting unstuck from an unhappy, unfulfilling life, they just cannot see a way out. They believe they're doomed to this joyless, anxious, or sad life. They believe what happened to them in the past or how they were raised has a hold on them, forcing the cycle of negative thoughts and sadness to continue. I believe that this is because they needed a different type of therapy to help with their healing process. This became abundantly clear to me during my employment as a psychiatric nurse in a group home for children. This was a residential setting where young children and teenage girls and boys lived, received intense therapy, went to school, and were not permitted to leave without a staff member accompanying them. They couldn't even use the bathroom alone. They were deemed a danger to themselves or others and needed a higher level of supervision than could be provided at home and in their home district school. Some suffered from severe mental illness, causing serious behavioral problems such as destruction of property, aggression, violence, and suicidal behavior.

These young people (residents) were admitted to the group home with the expectation that they would comply with the program, which involved acknowledging and working through their trauma. The facility was one that practiced trauma-informed care. In theory, this was a great plan. In reality, not so much. It was difficult to implement for several reasons. Topping the list were the lack of staff buy-in, staffing shortages causing unsafe situations, and the severe behaviors of the residents causing burnout (for both staff and residents). I was never certain what I would be hit with when walking through the door. I mean that both literally and figuratively. I took my fair share of slaps and punches, received a pretty powerful kick to the ribs (that was fun, no deep breaths for weeks), and lost a fistful of hair (that pissed me off the most) among other things. So, treatment shifted toward the illness model, focusing on trauma instead of resilience. Some people need to process their trauma in depth before they can move forward because the trauma was severe and sometimes delayed reactions to past trauma can occur later in difficult situations. Others do not need to process the trauma they experienced in such depth. They become too stuck on it to move forward. They need to acknowledge it, receive validation for their feelings, and then focus on their resiliency to move forward. If adequately prepared in this way, they can find the strength to deal with it if it resurfaces during future stress. These needs should be determined, and each patient should be treated individually with the appropriate type of therapy, as there is no cookie-cutter treatment for mental health issues.

It's possible that psychiatry as a discipline has gone too far regarding treating trauma. We question every difficult emotion to see if it was caused by some past trauma, forcing our patients to focus more on the trauma or the possibility of trauma rather than their resilience, what is good in their lives, and how to move forward. I believe we may have overcorrected and driven the pendulum the other way. What a shame. It's possible this has contributed to the mental health epidemic we're currently experiencing, especially in young people. A focus on resiliency would no doubt help this problem. But it's not just psychiatry that's guilty of this overcorrection.

In the 1990s, when my husband completed his medical residency, the standard of care was to ensure that patients experienced adequate control of their pain. The belief at the time in primary care was that pain was not well controlled. Managing pain became as important as managing temperature, blood pressure, and respiratory status (the three vital signs). In fact, assessing one's level of pain became the fourth vital sign. But medicine went too far. They overcorrected and caused an epidemic of addiction. Now, physicians are hesitant to prescribe pain medication for fear of creating addicts, another overcorrection that perpetuates the cookie-cutter treatment model, leading to poor outcomes for patients.

It seems that many social reform programs follow the same model. Instead of fixing a problem, we create another. We help some, but in the process, we leave many struggling with a new problem that's worse than the one they sought help for. The fix can be a slippery slope that's difficult to deice.

Please understand that I believe severe trauma must be processed to move past it. However, there is a fine line between processing and reinforcing the trauma. When do we leave the past in the past and work on moving forward? If you've been in therapy for years and feel that you haven't made progress and aren't feeling stronger or learning emotional regulation skills, coping skills, and techniques to help life be better, then it's time to reevaluate the therapist-client fit and consider making a change. It's possible you need some help finding and tapping into your resilience. Or you may need a new treatment plan. Remember, you're in charge. Advocate for yourself. No one knows what you need better than you. Others may be better trained to help you get there, but only you know what you need.

An example of an excellent individualized treatment plan, although accidental, is that of a fifteen-year-old female patient who struggled with anxiety, depression, poor self-esteem, and suicidal thoughts who was being discharged from the group home. Our interactions mostly centered around the medications she took or didn't wish to take and her ability to maintain control over the things she was to do or not do in the program. I would remind her of her strength and ask her if focusing her energy on the problem was helping her. I asked her if she thought it would be more helpful to concentrate her energy on what could be done about the problem. On the day of her discharge, she said to me, "Thanks, Nurse Maria. You don't give up on anybody."

I took her words to heart, and they became a driving force for me to help the patients I serve move forward toward a better life. That young girl changed my life more than I changed hers. She was one of the few who didn't reenter the system later. She refused to focus on her past trauma in therapy because she didn't believe she needed to. She discovered her resiliency. My profession needs to be better at helping our patients find their resiliency and use it to move forward past their trauma.

Working at the assisted living facility was supposed to be very easy for me since I had experience as a nurse in a residential setting. I love and respect the elderly population, and I find it easy to connect with them on many levels. There is much to be learned from them and their life experiences. The job was supposed to be part-time, which would allow me to focus on my studies. I was never so wrong. The director of nursing was fired (this was a good thing), and I was asked to fill the position, as I was the only RN and there was no one else to fill her shoes. I could either abandon ship or suck it up and be part of the change I wanted to see for the elderly at the end of their life. So, I accepted the challenge, and I met the loveliest and the crotchetiest of elderly individuals. Many were sad that they couldn't live alone or with their families any longer, as they needed more care than they were able to get in their previous homes. So many of them were severely depressed and unhappy, and many felt hopeless. They couldn't see the value in life. They were sad that their lives didn't turn out the way they wished. They thought and spoke of this day in and day out, reliving the sadness daily. They were stuck, deeply stuck.

In all the places I worked, I noticed that something was missing. All these individuals received therapy, some of which was intense therapeutic treatment with medication and behavior management. But they all had one thing in common. The patients all felt like they were stuck. Even while receiving treatment, some thought that their current situation was their life and that they would always be flawed and managing their symptoms. Either they felt they didn't deserve to be happy or had suffered so long that they just gave up trying. They were overwhelmed. They allowed their past and what happened to them or did not happen for them to dictate their future. Their belief system was flawed. The revolving door continued to turn. In fact, it spun like a merry-go-round minus the fun.

Something was missing, and I believed it was a failure not on the part of these individuals but something bigger. A failure that these individuals couldn't see coming since they relied on the system to help them get unstuck. But sometimes the system didn't provide an effective fail-safe, a backup plan to handle the possibility of the return of symptoms and mitigate the damage. Upon discharge from a facility, patients are provided with outpatient therapy, a case manager, a month's supply of medication, and referrals for whom to contact if symptoms return. These are necessary components of treatment plans. However, more focus should be placed on moving forward, on recognizing resilience, and on the strengths patients already possess. These ideas should be part of the treatment plan from the start. It's the job of the mental health professional to help patients find resiliency no matter how bad things are. Sometimes this is not the case because work on processing the trauma comes first. I believe it should be simultaneous.

The young people needed to believe that their situation could change. And believe me, some situations were really bad, but that was all the more reason to find and develop resiliency. They needed to change their focus. They needed someone to remind them of their strength. They needed to appreciate what was going right instead of solely on what was wrong. Yes, their symptoms needed to be managed, and they needed to understand what happened to them, but they also needed to acknowledge that what happened to them did not dictate who they were and that they could be who and what they wanted. They needed to believe that they were worth the effort and that their past happened but didn't continue to happen unless they allowed it to.

What the elderly individuals needed was someone to help them remember all the positives and good they did in their lives. They needed therapy that could help them focus on and recall what was wonderful in their lives. They needed to focus on the fact that they were safe and well—that they had someone managing their health care and daily activities and to take them where they needed to go. They needed to view their situation differently. They needed to develop new relationships and see the value in this. It's never too late to form a bond with another individual, as evidenced by the Harvard Study on Adult Development.[20] More about this important study will be covered in a later chapter.

What every one of these individuals did not understand is that happiness, satisfaction, and contentment are internally generated. These feelings cannot be gained from external forces. Happiness is a decision we make, not something that someone else can provide for us. No one can make us feel anything. No one can tell us how to feel or how we should respond to events that happen to us. We decide to feel a certain way, and we can decide whether we can be happy or unhappy. We decide where we place our focus. Our current situation is what we decide it is. Nothing is either all good or all bad, and whether it is good or bad is an opinion, not a fact. In the words of the Greek philosopher Epictetus, "Men are disturbed . . . not by things that happen, but by their opinion of the things that happen."[21] Our actions are the result of what we think, so be careful how and what you think.

Shit happens, but how much you decide to focus on it is a choice. It's a choice to be a victim of life circumstances or a survivor of them. You can choose to move past the shit instead of dwelling on it. The difference is that those who give all their attention to their problems instead of to the solutions will keep the problem alive and kicking—kicking their ass. They perpetuate their own unhappiness. Those who see their problems as temporary and envision solutions kick ass and move past the problem. They use everything available to them to fix it. They can see the other parts of their life, the good parts, and give these more of their attention. You can do this too. Start right now and think about what you should leave in the past, what you should not keep alive to kick your ass. You can decide that although what happened has already happened, it doesn't have to keep happening.

Your brain will focus on whatever you tell it to. It will help you keep the problem alive or form new patterns of thinking, ones that will help you move forward and past the problem to the wonderful, happy life ahead of you. But you must tell it to change focus to what is going well and what has gone well in the past. You must think of these things more than you think of your problems. Then you must view your problems in terms of what you can do to make them better. You can do this. It's not difficult. It just takes focus. Start focusing on what's good in your life and be thankful for it. This is the basis of the PAT method.

I used to think I was a bad test taker, since I did poorly on standardized tests in school. I won't ever disclose my SAT scores. I just
thank the universe that my results weren't the only consideration for
acceptance to college. Even in college, I sucked at testing. Therefore, I
believed I would do poorly on every test I ever took. My belief drove
my actions. I started every test with worry and anxiety, which made
my faulty belief become a reality. My actions followed my thoughts
because, as Dr. Maltz reminds us, that is how the brain works.[22] I
made my negative belief a reality and let it deprive me of what I
wanted so badly to do. I had wanted to go to nurse practitioner school
many years ago but kept dismissing the thought because I believed I
would never pass the state certification exam. I refused to believe that
because others had passed it, I could pass it. I allowed my negative
bias to rob me of my dream. Instead of getting a master's in nursing
to be a nurse practitioner, I got a master's degree in business because
I didn't have to take a state certification exam. But I didn't really want
an MBA. I wanted a master's in nursing!

I have since learned that my belief was faulty. It was just an opinion, my opinion, and that didn't mean it was correct. I decided to
focus on my strengths instead of my weaknesses. I'm now a nurse
practitioner because I changed my belief system. I chose to do that.

It's never too late. Correct your faulty belief system now so that
you can enjoy your life from this moment forward.

I ended up with an MBA that I don't need, but I didn't view it as
a mistake. I viewed it as a success that I could recall when I needed to
gain confidence to get my MSN. I might never have gotten my nurse
practitioner certification if I didn't realize that I could earn a master's
degree. Because I was successful at the MBA, I could be successful
at an MSN. My brain was like, *Been there, done that, can do it again.* I
changed my view of testing and learned to study a different way. My
belief changed, and my actions followed. There were many tests, and

I passed them. I use that and the MBA as positive thoughts to help my brain form power pathways. I also have a feeling that the MBA may be even more useful to me in the future. I have no idea what the future holds, but I know what I want it to.

POWER PATHWAYS

Think about things in the past that have gone well for you or that have made you happy. Thinking of these things and allowing yourself to reexperience them is a great place to start. Dr. Maltz shares that recalling positive events and allowing yourself to reexperience them builds and strengthens neural pathways that can help you maintain a positive outlook on life.[23] The more you use these power pathways, the stronger they get. You don't have to worry about breaking the negative thought pattern. Just work on replacing it with the positive, and the negative will fall out of favor in the brain and disappear.[24] It's essentially pushed out by the positive. Whatever we choose to focus on is what the brain makes use of. Make use of the power pathways. In the words of Richard Buckminster Fuller, brilliant engineer and inventor, "You never change things by fighting the existing reality. To change something, build a new model that makes the existing model obsolete."[25] We can build new positive thoughts that replace and make our old negative thoughts obsolete because they're of no help to us anyway. End the negative thought process and begin a new positive way of thinking because, in the words of T. S. Eliot, "The end is where we start from."[26] Change your opinion. Change your story. Start today. Don't wait for things to get worse.

CHAPTER 3

THE BRAIN—NOT JUST ANOTHER ORGAN

"Whether you believe you can do
a thing or not, you are right"[27]
—*Henry Ford*

The brain is so powerful that if you choose to think negatively or believe that you cannot do something, you will be right, and your brain will be very, very good at helping you not do it. But if you believe you can and intend to do so, your brain will help you achieve it. We'll discuss this in more detail later. But for now, just know that the power of the brain and nervous system is miraculous, so miraculous that some have difficulty believing its potential.

Neurons, which are nerve cells in the brain, transfer information to each other via neural pathways at speeds around two hundred miles per hour.[28] But the brain wields so much more power than just speedy processing. Have an open mind and you will learn what you can do to control your own life instead of merely existing and getting through.

I have counseled several pregnant and new mothers who have asked me why they have had the horrible thought of dropping their babies while going down the stairs. Some even take the thought further and think, *What if I threw my baby down the stairs?* This is obviously a terrifying and horribly disturbing idea. But they're not bad or freakish for thinking it. People sometimes believe the thought is a premonition of something that may happen or something they might do. This gives power to the thought, and it continues to enter or intrude on their regular thoughts. As Winston and Seif explain, the more one tries to fight it, the more the idea shows up and gets tangled in our brains.[29] Then the brain overreacts, entering high-alert mode. It sends signals to the nervous system to watch out. Now, when the thought enters the brain, it sparks panic. The brain is trained in a way that when this thought comes, the result is anxiety and panic. It misinterprets small incidents as large ones that require immediate action.[30] Since it has always done this and has had no opportunity to develop or strengthen positive power pathways, the brain does what it has always done—whatever it takes to get rid of the thought. Afterward, all future similar thoughts elicit the same response, and the brain sends messages that we should avoid things and events that may cause this feeling.[31] And so, we miss out on things we want to do out of fear of the thought actually coming true, which makes the thought even more powerful, allowing it to have control.

Sometimes, even things or thoughts that did not previously produce anxiety may elicit discomfort or even panic if they are associated with the fearful thought, and the cycle continues.[32] For example, if a woman had the fearful thought of dropping her baby while walking down the stairs, she might avoid the stairs altogether from then on. Now, the negative intrusive thought is in control of her life. This loop continues because some people are afraid to say what's going on in their brain for fear of being shamed; committed; or, even worse, having their child taken away. If not for the stigma, lack of insurance, or lack of access, they could receive helpful information to reduce their symptoms and begin to feel better. There are laws to protect people from being hospitalized or treated against their will. For this to happen, one must either be deemed a danger to themselves or others, or be unable to survive on their own in the community and have no one to assist or be responsible for them.[33]

Information is power. If everyone only knew how common and fixable the problem was, they would not feel like a freak or a bad person, or have guilt that they suppress because thinking of it is too terrible for them to tolerate. If the strange thought is treated like the weird, strange idea that it is and dismissed as such, it loses power, and the control it was believed to have disappears. Then, instead of feeling freakish for having the thought, the person can take control and eventually be able to extinguish it altogether. If their sadness or anxiety is faced and addressed, they can get unstuck. We obsess about strange thoughts or mistakes and cause them to get stuck in our brains, but we can stop the cycle of feeling shame, guilt, or unhappiness. We can choose to learn how. This is not difficult, but it involves practice and habit formation. As Peace Pilgrim once said, "If you realized how powerful your thoughts are, you would never think a negative thought."[34]

COGNITIVE BIAS

Cognitive bias is a term that describes the thought patterns we have that are incorrect or stuck in the negative pathway. People suffering from anxiety and people suffering from depression have something in common: they tend to have a negative bias to their thoughts and words. They think negatively, which causes them to act in accordance with the negative thoughts. They're always looking at the wrong side of things. Their focus is perpetually on what has gone wrong instead of what they learned from it and how to make it right. There is no forward movement or progress. They are stuck where they are, and they stay there because this is what has always happened. They believe things won't work or go right because things never have. This belief prevents them from trying new things. This is a faulty belief system that limits them from finding true happiness because what we think controls what we do, and if we think we can't, we don't try, so we don't achieve.

Negative thinking leads to "what-if" thinking. As if negative thinking wasn't enough of a problem, some people compound their issues by creating scenarios that don't exist. They create more things to worry about, and these things usually end up not happening. Negative pathways are strengthened by the constant worry about things that could happen. The more we think of these things, the more our brains become accustomed to them, and they become part of our belief system. Then, the belief becomes a reality that we feel the need to respond to. Dr. Maltz refers to this as "fighting straw men."[35] We struggle with things that aren't there or haven't happened because we fear they might happen. By doing this, we strengthen the negative pathways, and when we need strength to get through something tough, all the brain knows is failure or negative consequences. And so, failure keeps happening, and then we quit trying. We create a monster in the form of negative thinking. But we can slay the monster with a positive mindset if we restructure our thoughts.

Remember, positive psychology is a type of psychology that points to the strengths and support people already have. It encourages people to focus on what's already good in life and uses this to remind them of their resiliency to help them move forward.[36] It gives them focus, a place to start, and direction. It helps them realize what they need to do now to feel better.

I use positive psychology in my practice. I help my patients realize that focusing on the past will not help them move forward; it will keep them in their limited world. I ask them to view their situation differently, as if they were looking in on someone else's life. I ask them to see the problem as a challenge that needs solutions and not the catastrophic event that their mind has created. I ask them to pretend that they're great at finding solutions to problems and assure them that I can help. I ask them to focus more of their attention on the parts of their life that are strong and good, and to use what they already have to correct their course. They create a list of what's good in their life that they can look at again and again. This isn't just merely thinking positively; as Dr. Maltz points out, positive thinking alone is futile unless belief follows.[37] You must believe that you have the power to change and that you can do it.

Martin Seligman, who is known as the father of positive psychology, catapulted the world of psychiatry to new levels with his theory that focuses on an individual's strengths to promote happiness and well-being instead of pathological conditions and symptoms like in the illness model.[38] He is also well known for his theory of learned helplessness, in which he explains that when people believe there is little chance for them to control or change their life, they stop trying. They give up and accept what they think they cannot change. Based on his own research, he also taught and wrote about his opposing theory of learned optimism.[39] Thank you, Martin Seligman. I am forever grateful.

Positive psychology is a type of therapy that helps one to find a starting point for change and identify the work they can do right now to see immediate results that will get better with time. It provides hope for a better way instead of sympathy for an illness they feel they might have. This type of therapy is more solution-focused than symptom-focused. Yes, it identifies how one feels, but it then quickly determines a path to wellness without focusing on symptoms or the *why* of the situation. This does not belittle anyone who has been participating in traditional therapy. It does not discount the pain and suffering. It only provides an alternative route for healing that helps one move forward. There is never just one way. There are different paths to wellness, and there is one for you.

Positive psychology is based on **resilience theory**.[40] This theory "suggests that [many psychiatric problems are] less about the events surrounding stressful times and trauma and more about our subjective experience" or how we view the events.[41] According to Dr. Jeremy Sutton, a researcher, writer, ultramarathoner, and psychologist who specializes in human performance and positive psychology, "Resilient individuals typically have specific characteristics, such as being able to regulate emotions, able to solve problems effectively, and maintain positive relationships. Such individuals also often have a strong sense of purpose and meaning, which helps them find hope and motivation in difficult times."[42]

The longest-running study about what strengths or qualities happy and healthy people possess is the Harvard Study on Adult Development. It started in 1938 and is still running. What sets happy people apart from those who are not happy? So many believe it's a great, high-paying job, while some say better work conditions or weekends off, but nope! The study revealed that it's strong close relationships with other people that keep people feeling happy and physically healthier. Dr. Maxwell Maltz supports this idea, sharing that "One of the most pleasant thoughts to any human being is the thought that he is needed, that he is important enough and competent enough to help and add to the happiness of some other human being."[43] However, he cautions us not to view happiness or this bond with others as a condition of our behavior, or a reward of some sort, because he believes this may lead to feelings of guilt over the desire for happiness.[44]

Dr. Jeremy Sutton agrees that "Resilience theory has important implications for psychotherapy, as it suggests that helping individuals develop resilience can be crucial in achieving positive outcomes."[45] Resilience is the ability to withstand stress and overcome problems using whatever strengths and support you have. Strong family ties or relationships help us feel connected to the support these individuals can provide. Knowing we aren't alone and that we have people on our side to guide us through tough times allows us to realize that we can get through whatever life throws at us.

I once had a young patient who referred to her brain as needing crutches. She experienced obsessive thoughts that interfered with her ability to enjoy anything. Her initial solution was "I can't, so I stopped trying." She has since learned that her solution was flawed and that her mistake was struggling and fighting with her obsessive thoughts. She was allowing them to control what she did or didn't do. She wondered why she was this way and why she had to work so hard to be what she referred to as "normal." That's all she wanted, to be normal. To not have these thoughts that controlled her. She allowed them to limit her. I reminded her that crutches were temporary and so was her situation. She learned in therapy that she could stop the cycle of anxiety, hopelessness, and frustration and lose the crutches. She now realizes that anxiety is just an emotion, a feeling that cannot hurt her and that she can control just like any other emotion. With help, she restructured her thoughts and changed how she viewed her situation using positive self-talk and visualization. Meanwhile, she appreciated the support from her loving family. Her family noticed the change soon after she started this therapy and scheduled weekly appointments far into the future for her. They noticed a major improvement in her self-esteem and mood and a decrease in her obsessive thoughts and actions. She also took medication to help her feel better while she learned the tools to help herself. She may be able to stop the medication soon, now that she has the tools to move forward. She realized her resiliency and used all that she had to improve her situation.

A sixty-eight-year-old woman entered my office anxious, depressed, and crying. She stated that since she'd seen her primary care doctor, who told her she had symptoms of Parkinson's disease, she hadn't been able to think of anything else. She was obsessed with the idea of having the disease, how it would change her life, and what would happen if it got worse. She spent her days searching the internet for information on the disease and was worried she would experience the symptoms she read about. She couldn't enjoy time with her family, her retirement, or her life. She was referred to a neurologist who told her that she couldn't be diagnosed with Parkinson's at the time, as her symptoms did not meet the criteria for diagnosis or treatment. Yet, she was convinced she had it. Her family insisted that she see someone.

She stated that this should be the best time in her life, as she was retired and spent her time watching her grandchildren. Her daughter was expecting another child, and she couldn't even be happy about it because she was so anxious and sad about her possible diagnosis. She agreed to therapy and an antidepressant, as she needed to do something to help her move past this situation. I suggested my positive therapy approach. I told her that she could waste more time Googling Parkinson's and continue to obsess and panic about a diagnosis that she didn't even have yet, or she could stop Googling, stop ruminating about something there was no evidence for, and focus on what was right in front of her. I reminded her of the things that strengthened her resiliency, such as her children, who brought her such joy; her beautiful grandchildren; her husband, who deserved her attention; and the life that she had been neglecting while focused on what was wrong in her life. I asked her to dedicate one month to focusing all her attention on her beautiful life and family and not waste another day of it—no Googling, no thinking about what might be, and no crying over what she couldn't control and had no evidence for. She said she would try. I asked her to make the decision to do it right there on the spot in my office. She asked, "Why right now?"

I informed her that the brain cannot process "I'll try." Is it doing it or not? What is "try?" The brain needs a firm "I will do this." She said she would and left my office.

She returned a month later for a follow-up visit to check on her progress with the medication and her new intention. She was feeling better, but she needed more work. We spoke of Parkinson's only to say that there are varying degrees of the illness and not everyone who is diagnosed with it is debilitated. We also talked about how there are new medications that delay the disease process so that some people don't even show symptoms and can enjoy life. Then we spoke of what would happen if she did get the diagnosis. Would she stop living and retreat to her room and lay in bed all day, or would she decide to live her life the way she wished to while appreciating all that it has to offer her? She went on her way to think more about what I said.

She returned in another month to tell me that her neurologist started her on a new medication to treat her symptoms and that she was hopeful that it would help her. She had been enjoying time with her grandchildren, and she told me of the new baby. She no longer Googled information about her possible condition and had accepted that if it is the case that she does in fact have Parkinson's, she will live her life to the fullest and not let one moment of apprehensive anxiety steal her joy and happiness. She was done wasting time worrying about worry. She had decided to no longer focus on what could be wrong and instead focus on what's so wonderful in her life. She decided to take medication and use positive therapy to control her thoughts and her life. She took charge! She changed her attitude to one of gratitude for all the good in her life. She involved her family and asked that they remind her when she slips into a negative mindset. She put the resiliency theory and the PAT method to work and noticed how simple it was to implement. She realized the profound results of her own power. Take note of the quote by Dan Millman: "You don't have to control your thoughts; you just have to stop letting them control you."[46]

There are many other stories like these in which people either don't have the right information or didn't have anyone take the time to explain that life doesn't have to be the way it has been if they don't want it to be. If they want a different life, they can have it. They can change their perspective, rewrite their story, and get unstuck. Believing that they could be happy and then focusing on the things that make them feel good is what starts the process. They can tap into what support they already have to increase and realize their resiliency. A little information goes a long way. Knowledge is power. We can be powerful if we choose to be. Choose power.

CHAPTER 4

MEDICATION—TO TAKE
OR NOT TO TAKE,
THAT IS THE QUESTION

"Medicine is not only a science; it is also an art. It
does not consist of compounding pills and plasters;
it deals with the very processes of life, which must
be understood before they may be guided."[47]

—*Paracelsus*

The decision to take medication is an individual choice. What might help one person may not help another. Trial and error is the norm in psychiatry. If one medication doesn't work well enough or causes too many side effects, then try another, and another until you find the right one for you. The next step is adjusting the dose incrementally until the right amount of medication is found. Patience is not only a virtue, it's necessary in psychiatry. But along the journey, there's much to be learned.

Part of resiliency is advocating for ourselves and tapping into those resources and supports we have. Patients and parents need to speak up to their providers. Don't worry about giving them too much information. Disclose everything. Hold nothing back. Holding back information may delay effective treatment. This is a safe space to speak your mind regarding your symptoms. What are symptoms? Symptoms are anything that's bothering you or interfering with your ability to live a productive, enjoyable life. Share everything, but identify the most prominent symptom. This provides your practitioner with a starting point, especially when medication is involved. Many medications can help several problems, and it's important to know all the symptoms to find the medication that will target the most while addressing the more bothersome ones. If you're uncertain of what symptoms you're experiencing, tap into your resiliency and bring a trusted close friend or relative who can support you and provide collateral information to help with your treatment. Often, these individuals see things we don't see in ourselves and can help pinpoint symptoms.

WHAT'S GOING ON?—THE PROBLEM

Some of the things you should be prepared to discuss with your psychiatric provider include the following:

- How long have you been feeling this way?
- How much time and energy are you devoting to managing the problem?
- Are you exhausted from the work you've been putting in to address or modify the problem?
- Does the problem negatively impact your relationships, your ability to form new relationships, or keep the ones you have?
- Do the symptoms impact your ability to do your job, schoolwork, or daily activities?
- Have you noticed decreased productivity or grades?
- Do you feel stuck in an unending cycle of frustration, irritability, sadness, or unhappiness?
- Are you able to enjoy family, friends, and significant others, or do you prefer to be alone and avoid others?
- How often do you isolate yourself from others?
- Are you unable to do the things that used to bring you joy?

- Do you feel overwhelmed when you must do something and instead just do nothing?
- Do you have difficulty getting out of bed to start your day?
- Have you noticed changes in your appetite, sleep, hygiene, or self-care?
- Do you often find yourself thinking of the worst-case scenario?
- Do thoughts pop into your head that feel disturbing? Do you wish you could stop them?
- Do you feel like hurting yourself?
- Do you compare yourself to others and feel like a failure?
- Have you tried psychotherapy, and did it help?
- Do you think to yourself, *I just wish I could feel better?*
- Do you have fears or beliefs that hold you back?
- Do you have fears about medications but wish you could at least try them?
- Do you feel that you should be able to get better without medication?
- Are you afraid that since you take other medications, you cannot take more?
- Do you know someone who had a bad experience with medications, and are you afraid this will happen to you?
- Are you afraid of addiction?
- Do you feel that taking medication would be giving up or giving in and there is no way to get off them?
- Are you afraid to reach out for help because you don't know what will happen?

WHAT IF THINGS COULD BE DIFFERENT?
- What have you got to lose?
- What would life be like if you didn't have this problem and you could be happier?

- What if you didn't have thoughts that held you back from being the person you're meant to be or want to be?
- What if medication could help you lift yourself out of the hole you're stuck in?

There are as many reasons why you should get help as there are fears and reasons why you shouldn't. Why not think of it in a different way? Why not change your thoughts to those that are more useful to you in getting where you want to be?

Can you do everything on your own? I don't know anyone who can. How have you solved past problems? When there's a problem in life, sometimes you hire a professional to fix it, right? When you need your house remodeled, you hire a contractor who knows how to navigate the world of construction. And guess what? This person cannot do it all either. They cannot be an electrician, plumber, carpenter, and mason. They need to hire subcontractors who are experts in other areas to do what they cannot do. Likewise, you are the general contractor of your life, but you cannot do it all. You need the expertise of others. We all do at times. I do, my patients do, and you do too. So, use what's available to you to improve your situation. You cannot be all things, and some things you cannot fix on your own. Know this and ask for help.

What if you cannot change your circumstances? And what if your unhappiness is a direct result of these circumstances? What if you feel you have nothing to be grateful for? Then be grateful for you, for being alive, and for your strength in dealing with your problem. Try to see your problem in terms of what you can do to fix it instead of seeing only the problem. Maybe you need some help figuring things out. Allow yourself to feel sad if that's what you feel, but don't live in that emotion. Nothing is beyond help. Nothing is impossible. You must decide that you will be happier. Seek help. Make a call. Reach out. Your local hospital has more services than you could imagine and can connect you. Do this for yourself. You're worth it. Be kind to yourself. Your future self will thank you. As J. P. Morgan said, "The first step towards getting somewhere is to decide you're not going to stay where you are."[48]

Help starts with a call. If you're uncertain where to find help and you have a primary care practitioner (PCP), then this is the first call you should make. They are a great resource for all things health related. They will either begin the process or refer you to a mental health specialist.

If you don't have a PCP, another good place to start is your local hospital or, if you have insurance, your insurance company. Ask what services are covered for a psychiatric evaluation. Get all the names of the providers who accept your insurance. Then, look at their qualifications. If your symptoms aren't significantly impacting your ability to function, then maybe you need to start with therapy and later see a psychotherapist. If your symptoms are negatively impacting your ability to function at your job or in your personal life, then you may need medication, which would require you to see a nurse practitioner, physician's assistant, or psychiatrist. Be sure to call them to see if they accept your insurance before scheduling the appointment. Providers enter and drop insurance plans depending on how many patients they have, insurance payments, and other administrative reasons. If you must wait too long for an appointment, schedule it, but continue to call around to see if someone can see you sooner. If you get a new one, cancel the first or you may be charged a fee because someone else will need the spot. If you must still wait longer than you wish, call your PCP to tell the office that you have an appointment but cannot wait for it to get help. They may start the process.

If you think you need both medication and therapy, you'll need to ask if the provider does both. Some nurse practitioners and psychiatrists do both, but some only do medications and, after prescribing, will refer you to a therapist. Regardless of what you need, you must start somewhere, and the decision to take medication can be confirmed by a practitioner, who will evaluate your symptoms and make professional recommendations.

Taking medication doesn't mean you're beyond help and must resort to other tactics. Rather, it's a way of using what's available to you to improve your situation. It doesn't hurt to have an evaluation to get the opinion of a professional. It could be one of the best decisions you've ever made. Many of my patients say that it is and share that they wish they made the decision sooner.

I treat a man who suffers from agoraphobia, which means he cannot do some of the things he wants to do because he has fears about being too far from his home. He stays fit and runs regularly. He has a beautiful attitude about life and loves people, and people love him. I enjoy seeing him and smile when I spot his name on my schedule. He would love to travel but cannot fly, as this causes too much anxiety. His world is limited. He came to see me about a medication he was prescribed in the past. It was a benzodiazepine, a controlled medication that he could take only when flying to relieve the anxiety of the flight but is not recommended for use on a regular basis. When I offered him medication that he could take on a regular basis to open his world up to more experiences, he said he felt that taking medication every day was giving in. I told him that I would prescribe the medication he asked for but that if he wanted to be able to enjoy more things and live a fuller life, he may want to consider other options. He was still not on board. I told him that I believed he was giving in anyway, but to his anxiety instead of the medication. I asked him how long he was willing to let his anxiety control his life. He took a few minutes to process my statement and then responded that he hadn't thought of it that way and that no one had ever put it in those terms.

He tried the medication and came back after his trip one month later expressing his happiness and gratitude that he could now travel the world with his wife and enjoy a fuller life. He made the decision to take back control of his life. He focused on a solution instead of on his problem. He changed his attitude and his world expanded, and he was grateful.

I also see a young woman who suffers from depression, which worsened after the birth of her baby. She had a traumatic childhood and didn't believe that she deserved true happiness. She was depressed to begin with, and then postpartum depression appeared and sucked out what little joy she had left in her life like a vampire. She dealt with her symptoms for so long that she just got used to them. She grew accustomed to feeling this way until it became her new normal. As she adapted, she slipped further and further away from normal until she had finally had enough. She came to see me when she realized that she could not see herself enjoying anything or anyone ever again. She couldn't go on feeling like she was, and she felt that her husband and baby deserved better. She was reluctant to take medication but finally agreed when I asked her what she had to lose. I asked her how long she wanted to go through this dark life. What if she could experience motherhood with her new baby the way she dreamed it would be? I don't try to convince my patients to take medication. I merely ask them what they think it would be like if they could enjoy the wonderful things in their lives.

HOW MEDICATION WORKS

Psychiatric medications don't put something in or remove something from your brain. They simply modulate the number of certain free-flowing neurotransmitters that already exist and are available for your brain to use. Neurotransmitters are chemicals in the brain that are necessary for the transport of messages between neurons or to other parts of the body. These messages are what enable your body to function. Without them, you wouldn't be able to eat, move, or even live.[49]

Medication is a trial-and-error process in psychiatry. If at first you don't succeed, try, try again. Sometimes medications don't work as well for some people as they do for others, possibly due to enzyme interactions. Some bodies process medication either too quickly or too slowly, or there could be an interaction that may cause more pronounced side effects. Some people need higher or lower doses than others. Your prescriber can see if your body is more compatible with certain drugs than others by ordering a genetic test. This involves a simple swab of your inner check that's sent to a lab to be processed. This test will show which drugs may be more compatible with your DNA and more likely to produce positive results and fewer side effects. It also indicates which drugs would likely not be a good match for you and should not be tried first. Thank you, brilliant scientists, for this informative and very helpful discovery!

The dose of a drug is determined by and adjusted based on a person's response to it—in other words, how much symptom reduction is achieved. If symptoms are partially relieved, meaning the person is somewhat better but could benefit more, then the dose can be increased. The increase is based on comparing side effects and benefits, as well as possible lab values and vital signs. All medications have potential side effects that *can* worsen as the dose is increased. Your prescriber will discuss the potential side effects and their severity with you before prescribing the medication. It's very important to communicate the presence of any side effects to your prescriber. Common minor side effects usually go away within the first week or so. If they do not, the medication can be changed, or another medication can sometimes be added to address the side effects that are bothersome but not serious. Oftentimes, stopping medication requires weaning, as some discontinuation side effects can arise if treatment is ceased abruptly. Your prescriber will tell you how to decrease the dose over time to mitigate the unpleasant effects of stopping a medication. Some people notice these unpleasant effects when they miss even one dose of their medication, so it's important to know what to do if doses are missed. Usually, you'll take the dose as soon as you remember missing it. However, if the next dose is due soon, you'll most likely need to skip the missed dose and take the next when it's due. This should be discussed with your provider.

Some people note the benefits of a drug sooner than others, depending on their metabolism, but generally, it takes approximately two weeks to notice any significant improvement. Many of my patients notice an improvement in symptoms during the first week, and then more improvement over the first month. Responses vary among individuals. However, feeling better is not a reason to stop the medication, as these treatments are not curative. They help control symptoms but do not make them go away permanently like an antibiotic does an infection. Generally, most providers will ask you to take the medication for at least one year. They will advise you on when and how to stop.

The first-line treatment for most of the conditions mentioned in this book that require medication is a group of drugs called selective serotonin reuptake inhibitors (SSRIs). This is medical jargon for drugs that modulate the amount of serotonin in your brain. Serotonin is a neurotransmitter in the brain—everyone's brain. It's responsible for helping to regulate our moods to help us feel better (as well as other things). This class of drugs is considered very safe for generally healthy people and can even be prescribed, if necessary, for pregnant or breastfeeding mothers and young children under close supervision by a prescriber. For those individuals with medical conditions, these drugs can be prescribed under closer supervision by your PCP and mental health prescriber.

Some commonly prescribed medications in this category are Prozac, Zoloft, and Lexapro. There are others, but these are the most frequently recommended and my favorites. They are especially good for treating depression, anxiety, obsessive-compulsive disorder, postpartum depression, and premenstrual dysphoric disorder. They can be life changing. These drugs are generally safe for long-term use provided you don't have any medical or other conditions that may prevent you from using them. However, there are a very few things that would prevent you from using one of these medications, such as certain bleeding disorders or cardiac, kidney, or liver conditions. Your prescriber will ask you about any medical conditions and determine if a medication is safe for you. You'll need to tell your prescriber about all your current medications and medical conditions.

The second class of medications to treat depression and anxiety disorders is the SNRI- category- serotonin and norepinephrine reuptake inhibitors. These medications modulate norepinephrine and serotonin. Norepinephrine is the neurotransmitter responsible for the fight-or-flight reaction and helps us pay attention and be alert for possible harm. It's the brain's built-in defense mechanism designed to protect us from danger and help us flee the scene if necessary. Some common medications in this category are Effexor, Pristiq, and Cymbalta. Just like SSRIs, this class of drugs is generally safe for long-term use, but they have side effects as well. Your practitioner will ask you about your medical history and medications you currently take, as well as check your lab values, blood pressure, kidney, and liver function. SSRIs and SNRIs are better tolerated than other classes of drugs, which is why they are initially chosen over other drugs for medication management.

Sometimes, a third-line medication is necessary if symptom reduction isn't adequate with the first two categories of medication. Tricyclic antidepressants are just as effective as SSRIs and SNRIs in treating depression, OCD, anxiety, and other conditions, but their side effects can be harsher. They also modulate serotonin and norepinephrine. These drugs are sometimes used alone, while other times, they are added to a medication that hasn't been entirely effective for the treatment of anxiety, depression, obsessive-compulsive disorder, or another diagnosis. Sometimes, two medications at lower doses are better in combination than one drug at high doses. This will be addressed by your prescriber and is a case-by-case decision.

These medications are called antidepressants, but don't let the name fool you. They're used to effectively treat many conditions. Some of the medications in this class can be used to treat migraines, insomnia, chronic pain, nerve pain, and bed-wetting in children.

A class of medications that's commonly used as an adjunct to SSRIs and SNRIs are antipsychotics. These medications are used in the treatment of schizophrenia and other conditions. Their classification sounds scary, but at lower doses, they're excellent choices for treatment-resistant depression, anxiety, or obsessive-compulsive disorder. They work quickly as helper medications to aid the initial medication in relieving symptoms. They primarily modulate the amount of the neurotransmitter dopamine in the brain's circulation. A few commonly used drugs in this class are Abilify, Rexulti, Vraylar, and Zyprexa. These drugs have a higher incidence of side effects that can affect your blood sugar, weight, and muscle movements, but do not let that scare you either. Your prescriber will monitor your lab values by ordering blood tests and asking you questions about how you're feeling. As long as these values are watched and kept within normal limits, these drugs can be safe, effective, and life changing.

NONDRUG TREATMENTS

Other noninvasive treatments are available and have minimal side effects. Transcranial magnetic stimulation (TMS), for instance, is a procedure where magnetic electrodes are placed on the scalp at strategic places mapped out by a specifically trained nurse practitioner, physician's assistant, or psychiatrist. TMS is not to be confused with electroconvulsive therapy (ECT). In TMS, the stimulus is delivered by a technician and the pulsations from the magnetic electrodes stimulate nerve cells in the brain. Treatments are approximately thirty minutes each, and usually five days per week for around four to six weeks. The benefits of this treatment are that it is not painful; can be used in place of medication; and has minimal side effects, which might include headache, dizziness, or tingling of the scalp. It is, however, time-consuming.[50]

The goal is to be happy and healthy by whatever method you and your practitioner decide. You do not have to live an unhappy life. You can change your life from this point on.

CHAPTER 5

What Do You Need to Change to Experience Happiness?

> " You cannot control what happens to you, but you
> can control your attitude toward what happens to
> you, and in that, you will be mastering change rather
> than allowing it to master you" [51]
>
> —*Brian Tracy*

So far, we've covered the *P*, which stands for past. You've heard some different strategies for how to leave the past behind. Now, let's move to *A*, which is for attitude. In the next few chapters, we'll cover how to adopt a more helpful and positive attitude. This step isn't about simply thinking positively, since that alone is good but not enough. It's about accepting what has already happened and adopting a more helpful way to think about the past and the present. It's a shift in attitude. This takes practice, but it's not difficult.

With a little help from someone who knows what you're going through, you can change, learn, and grow. You can begin a new chapter or rewrite your whole story. View what happened in the past through a different lens. Instead of believing that you are a certain way because you were raised that way and cannot change who you are, think, *I was raised this way, but I have learned that another way is better, and so, I chose to be this way, a new way.* No one is a victim of their past. No one should feel forced to stay stuck where they do not want to be. No one is holding you back. You are holding yourself back. Your belief about yourself is that you are stuck and that things cannot change. This is your opinion, and that is OK if you are OK with where you are right now. If not, then it's time for a change, a shift in attitude. But you must believe that you can change and use whatever is available to you, such as therapy, medication, and other tools. Use what happened in your past to make you more resilient. You may have made it through some tough stuff. You are stronger because of what happened. Start thinking about how strong you have become. Some would say that this isn't easy. I say it's not difficult either. You have the power to learn the tools that can help you help yourself. The following tools are simple, and you can start using them today. Practice is the key to success, and repetition is the mother of all learning. I use repetition in my practice to help my patients remember important details when a lot of information is covered in a short time. You will read things in this book that you have read in earlier chapters. This is intentional and will help you easily recall important information laid out in this book, as you may put it down and return to it at a later time. With a little practice, you can take charge of your emotions and reclaim your happiness. Keep reading to learn more.

GROUNDING BREATHS

To calm yourself, start with grounding breaths. I tell my patients to take three deep breaths, in through the nose and out through the mouth. Breathe in for a count of four. While breathing in, feel the air filling your lungs and picture it in your mind. I like to use the image of puffs of blue, windy air filling my lungs, almost like what you see in a cartoon. Then, feel the air go out of your body to the count of four, and with it any feelings of anxiety you are experiencing. Watch it leaving your body in your mind. Again, I "see" the blue puffs of wind leaving my body through my mouth. Do this three times with positive self-talk in between each breath. Tell yourself you're in control of your emotions, you can calm yourself, and you intend to be calm. Between the next breaths, tell yourself that you're feeling calmer. You're doing it, and you can feel the calmness. Focus on the feeling of calmness. Picture yourself sitting calmly, doing what you love to do to relax. After the third breath, tell yourself you did it. You calmed yourself because you intended it. If you're not as calm as you would like, continue the breathing process. Continue to view the mental picture in your head of you engaging in the thing that you do to relax. Make it a detailed picture. You're wearing the clothes you relax in, and your setting is where you always sit to relax. Notice the things in the environment. Do not focus on the negative. Do not tell yourself you can be less anxious or make the anxiety go away. Your words should remain positive and focus on the feeling of calmness. This type of breathing serves two purposes. First, it sends much-needed oxygen to your cells to lower your heart rate and blood pressure, which are typically elevated when anxious. This helps you to feel calmer. But just as importantly, it stops the negative thoughts for a minute and allows your brain to reset. Dr. Maltz refers to relaxation as "nature's own tranquilizer."[52]

One of my patients has postpartum depression and anxiety. She is breastfeeding and doesn't wish to take medication. There are medications that are safe to use during pregnancy and breastfeeding, but she would rather not take anything, and that is her decision. I respect it. Her baby is normally a source of happiness and serenity for her, except when he's crying. The crying triggers anxiety for her, but she's learning to change her reaction. She uses behavioral techniques to calm herself. When it happens, she immediately uses grounding breathing, positive self-talk, and visualization to calm herself. She's changing her perspective of the cries from that of an alarming situation to one of a cry for attention. She is working on changing her attitude toward her baby's cry to one that is more helpful for her and her baby. She views it as a call from her baby to be with her. She imagines herself sitting calmly, holding her baby, and spending sweet bonding time with him. She is doing well with this technique and is feeling better. It's still a work in progress.

COGNITIVE RESTRUCTURING—ASSESS THE DAMAGE

Next, you'll change your view of the situation, just like my patient in the story you just read. You can do this because you're in control of your emotions. Cognitive restructuring is a technique that therapists use to help people see a different way to think about things that are causing them to be stuck. What if it wasn't so bad? What is the real damage? How much does this event negatively impact your life today, tomorrow, next week, next month, or next year? If it doesn't change the way you'll act or live, let it go. Release it to the universe and focus on what's right in front of you. What if this thing that happened was meant to happen to give you direction and information on how to move forward? After having experienced what doesn't work, you now have guidance to proceed in a better way. Tell yourself, *Thanks, mistake*, for pointing you in the right direction. Now you know what not to do. Mistakes are lessons that drive change.

I'm not talking about severe trauma here. I'm talking about the things that happen in life that people cannot let go of that keep them from enjoying life, things that could be viewed differently. Changing how we view our situation will go a long way in determining our happiness. Some people cannot be happy because they see others as more successful and, therefore, happier. If we compare ourselves to those who live a different life, we set ourselves up for failure. This causes an inaccurate belief system of *I cannot be like that*, which is not on par with what we want to be or do in life. When we do this, we have already set ourselves up to fail with a faulty belief system. Forward progress is inhibited, and we become stuck. Do yourself a big favor and stop comparing yourself to others. You have your own strengths, even if you haven't found them yet.

Perhaps you have anxiety in social situations and constantly worry about saying or doing the wrong thing. We all say and do things we wish we had not. Tell yourself, *This cannot hurt me in any way. It doesn't matter.* Use the second step in the PAT method, change your attitude to one of acceptance, and move on. Don't waste your precious energy on things that don't matter. Focus your attention on what does matter. This is a much better use of your time and energy.

Maybe you worry whether your friends like you or are just being nice and tolerating you. Or maybe you think they just feel sorry for you and include you in their social plans for this reason. Recognize that this is your opinion and not a fact. Change your way of thinking about these things. Realize that they may not be true, and that it's possible to see another perspective, and then notice when the new perspective is confirmed. Notice when you're enjoying their company and when they are enjoying yours. Use the second step in the PAT method and be grateful for your friends and the ability to enjoy their company. Tell yourself, *I am a likable person. I am kind, and people like to be around me. They like my company and invite me to their functions because I am fun to be around. I can relax and enjoy them. I deserve to have fun.*

Maybe you're sad, and you feel like nothing ever goes right for you or everything is hard for you. This is a false belief and a negative bias. Change your thoughts to more helpful ones such as, *I intend on having a good day today. It's going to be a great day. I will get things done today.* Be specific about the things you want to get done. Break your tasks down into smaller parts that you can successfully tackle, and then allow yourself to feel productive. Feel the success of completing that part. Think of past things that you did well, achievements you made, or times when things went well. Be grateful for those times.

After you're done, enjoy the good feelings they bring to mind. Allow your brain to experience productivity. Do not focus on what you did not achieve. Instead, remind yourself of what you did and that you will get something else done tomorrow. Do this until you accomplish what you need to.

Trust me on this. When you believe you can do something, there's nothing that can stop you except you. Only your negative thoughts can prevent you from succeeding at your goals. Dr. Maltz finds that a habit can be formed in three weeks, but he also shares that there is one caveat; you must believe you can, or your actions will not be aligned with someone who can.[53] The more you tell your brain you can, the more it believes you can, and the sooner success will become your reality.

So, give this principle three weeks. You have nothing to lose by trying. If you don't try, then you will continue living the life you're living. It's your decision. Time will pass either way. So, why not use it wisely? As Shannon Kaiser says, "Your desire to change must be greater than your desire to remain the same."[54] You cannot expect to change if you do nothing. So, why not make a change and believe in yourself?

Dr. Maltz cautions that if you believe you are someone who can't, then you won't because you will continue to act like someone who can't. Your negative bias will come into play every time and prevent you from achieving what you want.[55] If your self-image is that of someone who has never had confidence or has never been able to do what they want to do, you must change it to that of someone who believes they can. Then you will, because you'll be doing the things that successful people do and acting like successful people do.[56] Dr. Wayne Dyer, therapist, professor at St. John's University, and author of many bestselling books, including *The Power of Intention*, shares that this mentality allows you to recognize the things that you encounter in everyday life that are beneficial.[57] People and circumstances are there, you just never noticed them before. Now you will start to notice the opportunities that are right in front of you that will help you achieve your goal.

The main difference between those who succeed at what they want and those who fail is the belief that they can. Their behavior is that of someone who can, and so they do. Take note of the poem "Thinking" by Walter Wintle:

> If you think you are beaten, you are
> If you think you dare not, you don't,
> If you'd like to win, but you think you can't
> It is almost certain you won't.
> If you think you'll lose, you're lost
> For out in this world we find,
> Success begins with a fellow's will.
> It's all in the state of mind.[58]

The mind is powerful. You have a mind and, therefore, you have power. Use it to your advantage.

MINDFULNESS

Just as this section's title suggests, be mindful of what's currently going on in your life. Focus on what's good in your life, what is going well, and what you can appreciate. This is called mindfulness. Do not dwell on what isn't going well. Look at what's wrong in terms of what you can do to make it right without dwelling on how bad it is. When you notice all the things that are good and right, your brain can help you figure out ways to make the other things better. You have solved problems in the past successfully. Recall those events and how you made them better. Reexperience them so your brain can strengthen its neural pathways and focus on success. When you think only of failure, that is all your brain has to work with, which is harmful. Noticing pleasant things that are happening in your daily life and thinking of things that make you happy in your everyday routine will allow you to shift your attitude.

POSITIVE SELF-TALK—YES, YOU TALK TO YOURSELF

Dr. Wayne Dyer suggests using positive affirmations and mantras to change the way we think and behave.[59] Dr. Maxwell Maltz agrees that by doing this, we can change negative thoughts into more beneficial ones that lead to success in life.[60] This strategy involves positive self-talk multiple times a day every day to keep your focus on moving forward. It might sound something like this: *I am good at my job, and I intend to get that promotion. My coworkers like me and my boss likes my productivity. I am a leader. I will be the leader of my team.* If you want to have more self-confidence, your mantra could be, *I am a confident, successful person who others respect and like. I intend to give a speech that is well delivered and well received. I can do this. I have practiced it with my family. If I can do it well for them, I can do it again for a group of clients at work tomorrow.*[61]

Use your mantra while you're recalling and visualizing past successes. Form a mental picture of doing what you want to do while telling yourself how good you'll be. It sounds like sci-fi, but trust me. Say your mantra every morning before getting out of bed, during breakfast, when you eat lunch, at dinner, and again before you go to bed.[62] If you forget to do this because you're not used to doing it, tie it to something you do every day such as brushing your teeth, combing your hair, getting dressed, or making dinner. Place a sticky note on your mirror so that you see it when you use the bathroom first thing in the morning.

VISUALIZATION

Next, you'll imagine yourself doing what you want to do and being how you want to be. Picture it in detail in your mind. This is called visualization, and it is an amazing technique that provides a positive experience that the brain can convert to memories and refer to later when you begin to do something you want to do. You see, as Dr. Maltz points out in his research, the brain doesn't care if you actually did the task or if you only imagined yourself doing the task. He shares stories in his research and writings proving that the brain doesn't make this distinction. It just doesn't care.[63] Therefore, you can provide it with images that can help you succeed. This is a technique used by Olympic, professional, college, and high school athletes. Sure, they practice, but they give the brain an added boost in the form of memories to perfect their skill. Corporate executives use visualization too, and some require their employees to engage in team-building exercises that incorporate these techniques to help them achieve successful outcomes and be better teammates.[64]

JOURNALING

Another technique some people find useful is journaling. Writing down things you're feeling is a good way to get them out and forget them if they bother you. It doesn't have to be a novel. A few lines are fine if you don't enjoy writing. I have a patient who does this when thoughts keep swirling around in her head and she cannot sleep. She writes them down before going to bed so she doesn't have to focus on them anymore. When thoughts are stuck, it may be helpful to write them down and then rip them up and throw them in the fireplace, trash, or shredder.

Journaling is also an effective way to focus on what's going well. Before bed, write down the things that went well during the day and what you are thankful for. This helps with mindfulness. Instead of rushing through your day without noticing the good stuff, take a minute to recall it and jot it down. Your brain will take it from there, and you will appreciate it later. Journaling is also good for ridding yourself of obsessive thoughts.

MEDITATION AND GUIDED IMAGERY

Many people use meditation or guided imagery to calm themselves or keep themselves in a positive mindset every day. There are many apps for both techniques. Guided imagery is a technique in which someone speaks softly, guiding your thoughts and images. Meditation can be done individually and requires a quiet place where you won't be disturbed so that you can obtain the best benefit. During meditation, some people focus on their breathing and relaxing their bodies while thinking calming, relaxing thoughts to declutter their minds. Most people set aside approximately thirty minutes for this, but even short meditations can provide benefits. If you don't have thirty minutes, just take a few moments to think of things that bring you peace. Those short moments, practiced several times a day, will benefit you in big ways.

These techniques can be used together in step fashion, individually, or in combination with others to address your symptoms. Your therapist will teach you how to effectively use them to reduce your symptoms, and then you can customize them to fit your needs and life. A good way to start is to use deep breathing before starting any of the techniques. This allows the brain to reset so it can focus on what you would like it to. The reset allows you to notice other more pleasant and helpful things when you open your eyes so you don't miss out on an opportunity to build a power pathway. It encourages mindfulness.

CHAPTER 6

DON'T MISS THE FOREST
FOR THE TREES

"A pessimist sees the difficulty in every opportunity;
an optimist sees the opportunity in every difficulty."[65]

—*Winston Churchill*

Don't be so focused on what's keeping you down that you miss what's right in front of you. Regarding negative experiences of the past, you can use what happened to you to strengthen your resilience. Let go of your struggle with the past and use the techniques discussed previously to rewrite your story. The attention we give to past negative events perpetuates unhappiness. This creates a vicious cycle of negativity, inaction, frustration, and sadness and causes one to feel stuck. Thinking of the struggle helps it live on and can create a situation where one feels like it is happening all over again each time it's recalled. Rethinking allows the negative pathways to become stronger. We don't want that. It happened once and will not happen over and over if you stop the thoughts from giving your brain fuel to strengthen the negative neural pathways. Let go of what's holding you down, and grab onto what can move you forward. Do some spring cleaning of your brain like you do your house. Get rid of old thoughts that no longer matter.

Negative focus keeps us where we are and prevents us from moving forward past the event to the beautiful things that lie ahead for us, such as new relationships, new experiences, or new jobs. We cannot experience those things if we refuse to allow ourselves to squeeze out of the hole we're stuck in. Dr. Maltz cautions us that this type of thinking may cause resentment.[66] Some people begin to resent others for their part in past negative events. They may even resent others for being able to enjoy their lives. This is a limiting mindset. It prevents us from developing and maintaining the relationships that increase resiliency. I did this, and it kept me stuck for too long. Do not limit yourself in this way. Focus on what you can do, not what you cannot. Focus your attention on how things can get better instead of how bad they are. You don't have to forget what has happened to you, but you can choose not to fixate on the events. You can choose to focus on what you have become and what you have yet to do. Do more of the things that bring you joy and less of what cause sadness. Decide to see a positive side. Make that decision right now. Leave the trees alone. Focus on the forest.

FEAR OF FAILURE

I was very unsure of myself as a child, teenager, and even young adult. I thought I had no talent, no real purpose, and that no one wanted to be around me. I thought my friends were just being nice to me. Alright, so maybe I was a bit annoying, but only because I worried about everything I said. I worried about saying something wrong or not saying or doing something. I focused on the trees instead of the forest. What if I hurt someone's feelings? The reasons just piled up until I couldn't remember what I was, or wanted to be, or do, or say. Geez, I was a mess. I had no self-confidence. I let others determine my self-image. If they said something about me, I made it true because I believed it. It became me because they said it. But why was it true? Who were they to me, and why did I believe them?

I was afraid to try anything new for fear of failure or embarrassment. I never told anyone about this, and I pretended that I was happy. But I wasn't happy. I was sad. I focused on what I thought I was and did nothing to become what I wanted. I missed out on the forest, all that life had to offer, because I focused on the trees, what I thought was my current situation.

The only thing that changed my life was that I chose to be happy. I didn't want to feel the way I was feeling any longer. I finally opened my mind to see what I was missing out on. I changed my perspective about things that happened and caused me to feel the way I did. I stopped believing things that weren't true and started believing in myself. I let go of the past, accepted what had happened, and became grateful for what and who I had in my life.

I have a young female patient who suffers from a type of obsessive thinking related to perfectionism. She couldn't enjoy her life due to her belief that everything she did had to be perfect. She missed out on so much of her life because she couldn't be happy with anything that wasn't, in her opinion, perfect. She could never live up to her own standards. She could never enjoy anything she did because it wasn't good enough. She held onto her resentment of this, and her brain never experienced the satisfaction of doing something right. She was always disappointed with what she did, so all her brain knew was disappointment. It formed negative pathways instead of power pathways. She missed the forest for the trees, until she'd had enough and decided to do something about it. She wanted to be as happy as those she saw around her. She decided to get help and she made an online appointment with my office. After her evaluation, she decided to use medication and therapy. She learned effective behavioral techniques to address her symptoms. She learned that "good enough" was more important than perfection.

The good-enough concept can be something we implement to decrease stress we're feeling, but it can also be used to enable us to feel success.[67] Good enough is an idea coined by Dr. Donald Winnicott, who was a psychoanalyst and pediatrician. He taught his patients that good-enough parenting was better than striving for perfect parenting skills, as striving for perfect robs children of learning how to adapt to independence while growing up.[68] It also robs parents of the enjoyment children bring. The concept of good enough applies to almost everything in life. Dr. Maxwell Maltz agrees with allowing things to be good enough.[69] Nothing has to be perfect.

Now this young patient of mine focuses on what she does well and enjoys her life. She may not always need medication since she's getting very good at behavioral techniques, but for now, she enjoys feeling good. She's allowing her brain to use the feeling of success to strengthen her power pathways.

HABIT EXTINCTION

A closed mind perpetuates negativity and maintains mediocrity and stagnation. An open mind encourages growth and paves the path to greatness. Open your mind to all that is available to you to help you in your quest for happiness. This isn't difficult. It just takes some practice and patience. You don't need to worry about extinguishing old habits. Instead, focus on starting new, more useful ones. The new habit will become preferred, and the old will wither away. Remember Richard Buckminster Fuller, the engineer and inventor whose advice was that it is better to build a new model to replace the existing one? This is true with **habit extinction**[70]—doing something in place of something else is all that's needed to rid yourself of a bad habit. Open your mind to use all that is around you to feel happy. Acknowledge how this changes your mindset and your life.

I was tired of my negativity and wanted to feel happy. I decided to shift my focus to what made me feel good. I extinguished the habit of reliving the experiences of my childhood that made me feel bad. They kept me angry and sad. My brain was doing exactly what I told it to. It was getting very good at recalling the information I was feeding it, so good that these thoughts became my go-to and were now in my forebrain for use whenever I needed them. But I never needed them. I never wanted them. Then why did they always pop into my head? Because I trained my brain to think of these negative thoughts, and it became a negativity champion. So, whenever I started to think of what made me sad, I immediately shifted my thoughts to what made me smile. For me, that was nature, animals, and my family. It took patience, but I did it. I stripped my brain of its old habit by just replacing it with a new, preferred habit. I became mindful of what was right in front of me. And you can too.

Mindfulness allows us to enjoy the moment and appreciate the small things that cause momentary happiness. The more we notice, the less momentary and more present the enjoyment is and the more patient and calm we become. Mindfulness is about seeing the forest instead of just the trees.

UMM, WHO'S NEGATIVE ENERGY IS THIS?

When anxious thoughts enter your mind for no known reason, don't feel guilty or judge yourself. Chase them away and tell yourself that you're OK and that there's no reason to feel alarmed. Say to yourself, "I'm fine." Then, breathe deeply, focusing on the breath going in, and exhale through your mouth, focusing on the air leaving your body. In between the breaths, tell yourself that you can calm down and that you're doing it right now, just as you learned in the previous pages. Note what's going on in your environment. Are others anxious or stressed? Is the negative energy yours or theirs? If it's not yours, excuse yourself and go to a quiet place. Move away from anxious, negative people. Don't allow soul-sucking vampire people to suck the energy from you. Tell yourself it's not your negative energy and that you are calm. You've likely heard the expression "Not my monkeys, not my circus." The same principle applies here. Push the negative energy back at the vampires. You have no responsibility to respond. Imagine this happening. Then visualize yourself as calm and comfortable.

Form the mental image of a protective bubble around you. The bubble repels all the negativities. You don't need to absorb the negative energy of others. Let them keep it. Don't encourage them to share by responding to it. This may sound like something a child would be taught, but it's a technique that adults find effective in aiding them to remain calm in a chaotic environment. Only you can protect your energy. You don't need to respond to the chaos. Give no eye contact to those who are part of the chaos. Ground yourself by touching objects in your environment that you can feel and identify while also noting the colors and patterns of things around you. Note that your feet are on the ground and you are steady. Feel them press into the ground. Feel any stress leaving your body. If you need to, do your three grounding breaths with positive self-talk. This allows your brain time to decide on the best course of action. It can decide that this is not an emergency, giving it time to activate the part of your brain that deals with rational thinking instead of overthinking.[71]

Dr. Martin Seligman has done a great deal of research on this topic. As the Director of the Positive Psychology Center at the University of Pennsylvania, he performed studies and discovered that both teachers and students were more successful when focus was placed on strengths and factors that increased emotional well-being.[72]

Dr. Maxwell Maltz also agrees with focusing on what's going well instead of what's going wrong. He reminds us that happiness is something we decide to do and "not something that happens to us."[73] Remember the Harvard University Study of Adult Development you read briefly about earlier? It's the longest-running study to date on happiness and health. It was started in 1938 and found that the biggest predictor of happiness was strong, connected relationships with other people. The individuals who had the "warmest connections"[74] with other people were the happiest and lived the longest. The study showed that these good relationships reduce stress and increase feelings of well-being. Stress negatively impacts mental and physical health. It can cause gastrointestinal distress, cardiac irregularities, headaches, muscle aches, immune dysfunction, and a slew of other physical conditions.[75]

Dr. Robert Waldinger advises that we strengthen relationships of all kinds. He suggests calling people we care about but have not spoken to in a while. In an interview by Molly Liebergall in February of 2023, Waldinger shares, "We talk about . . . this idea of social fitness. We mean it to be analogous to physical fitness. Physical fitness is an ongoing practice: I don't go to the gym today and then come home and say, 'Good. I'm done. I don't ever have to do that again.' The same is true with relationships."[76] He further explains that if you don't have strong relationships with anyone or just don't have anyone in your life, volunteer service can help you develop purpose and feel fulfilled. It's also a place where relationships can spark up.[77]

When we strengthen relationships, we develop a sense of shared strength that enables us to feel more confident and resilient. Unfortunate things that happen can be "shared," and the burden is often reduced because of the support we find in our close relationships. We don't feel as if we must handle things alone. This often ignites a sense of power over our lives because problems don't seem as big when we have support. Problems don't become catastrophes because we have others to help us look for solutions. This tends to shift the focus to solutions rather than the problem.

TRIGGERS

I hate that word. Talk about focusing on the problem! The term was originally coined to describe things that cause us to feel anxious, feel depressed, or obsess about something because they remind us of things that did this in the past. It refers to an event, a word, or something we experience or see that evokes in us an undesired emotional response. Fixating on the trigger as a trigger encourages focusing on the trees and not the forest. We miss the bigger picture and focus only on the trigger. We miss what else is going on around us. This term is very overused and has morphed over the years to include anything that pisses us off. This isn't what it was meant to describe. Allowing ourselves to feel triggered by things that we react negatively to keeps us limited because it encourages focusing on the past, past feelings, and what's going wrong instead of solutions and strengths. We can decide not to feel triggered. We can decide to adopt a different perspective of the situation.

I encourage anyone who's triggered by something to view the trigger as simply something someone said or did that does not apply in any way to them. If we're reminded of past trauma, we should view the trigger in terms of how we overcame it and the resilience it has produced in us. I caution you not to allow the words, actions, or opinions of others to have any impact on your well-being. You don't need to respond. You can choose not to. You can choose to use your protective bubble and other techniques to repel the negative energy of others back to them as discussed earlier. You can choose to see that others have different opinions and beliefs that you don't have to agree with. But these differing opinions don't constitute a trigger, and they shouldn't make you feel you should act or prevent you from acting the way you normally would. Don't let a focus on the negative details prevent you from being you or doing the things you want to do.

Have you ever worried about accomplishing or being good enough at something that you focused so much on the minor details that you were never able to start? Perhaps you get too bogged down with starting something, such as saving money, and become so overwhelmed by it that you don't even begin. Or maybe you're too focused on losing a certain amount of weight and think that it's too much, so you never start with the first pound. Or maybe there's too much focus on one issue in a relationship, superseding the good things about it, and you forget why you originally fell in love with the person. These are just a few common examples where people have allowed a negative bias, trigger, or inaccurate belief to get in the way of their happiness. I have done this professionally, personally, and socially. I have not pursued professional certifications or degrees (remember the MBA I didn't really want from chapter 2?), avoided personal relationships, and passed up athletic opportunities that would have made me happy if I had chosen to see the forest instead of the trees. I learned later that I didn't have to have such a narrow view of things. I learned how to have a broader perspective and imagine what I could do if I stopped focusing on the details that prevented me from trying. More about that in chapter 8.

CHAPTER 7

IMAGINE YOURSELF HAPPY

"It's a funny thing about life, once you begin to take
note of the things you are grateful for, you begin to
lose sight of the things that you lack."[78]

—*Germany Kent*

Now, after letting go of the past and allowing yourself to see the
forest (not just the trees), your mind is open. In this chapter, I'll
expand on those ideas and discuss even more ways you can be open
to what's around you, including the cues from the universe you might
not have seen before.

Another study done by Harvard University involving visualization used two groups of people who had imaging devices attached to
their heads to monitor their brains. One group was instructed to play
notes they were taught on the piano. The other group was asked to
simply imagine themselves playing the same notes. When the imaging device was reviewed, it showed that the same areas of the brain
were activated for both groups and that imagined practice improved
skills. This study provides evidence that the brain does not differenti-
ate real activity from imagined activity.[79]

In his book, *Psycho-Cybernetics*, Dr. Maltz provides the following example to further support this theory. Arthur Schnabel was a
renowned concert pianist who used visualization to practice, as he
loved to play but hated to practice. Who could blame him? He was

very successful with this method of "practice" because he believed he could be an accomplished musician.[80] Dr. Maxwell Maltz refers to this technique as "synthetic experience."[81] Schnabel provided his brain with the experience of repeatedly imagining playing the piano, which was as effective for him as physical practice.[82]

Visualization with piano practice is just one example of how powerful our imagination is and how it can affect outcomes in our lives. This applies to your happiness too! It's not just wishful thinking. There's science behind why visualizing your own happiness works. By imagining yourself happy, you're actually *creating* that happiness. I'll share a few more examples of how this works.

Dr. David Hamilton, a biochemist and a researcher at the Lerner Research Institute in Cleveland, supports this concept of the power of the brain as well. He shares the results of a study at the institute involving finger strength. Participants in two groups were asked to exercise one finger. However, one group was told to only imagine they were exercising the finger, while the other group physically performed the exercise. They found that the results were very similar. The group who physically performed the exercise increased their finger strength by 53 percent. The group who visualized the finger exercise increased their finger strength by 35 percent.[83] When concepts are learned, neural pathways are strengthened, and the task becomes easier. This is the theory behind the concept of muscle memory that you're probably familiar with. It isn't the muscles that are remembering, it's the brain.[84] We can all use this idea to strengthen neural pathways to improve our mood and change our situation.

Dr. Hamilton took this concept further, believing that we can use this type of visualization for healing. He spoke with many individuals who practiced the technique to achieve healing, and he believes that others can attain the same results.[85] Dr. Hamilton explains that healing can occur physically or emotionally.[86] "Visualisation works because it causes changes in the brain," says Hamilton. "In some ways, the brain doesn't distinguish between a real movement and an imaginary one. Studies show approximately the same neural changes when comparing real against imagined movements . . . imagined movements essentially give the body (and brain) a work out."[87]

The concept that Dr. Hamilton is referring to is called neural plasticity. This is a pattern of growth in the brain in which it changes neural pathways to accommodate newly learned concepts or experiences. When this occurs, there's an increase in the production of "synaptic connections."[88] Synapses are areas where information is exchanged between neurons and communication between brain regions occurs. This is how the brain tells the body to move, act, or think. The brain can convert new experiences from short-term to long-term memories by strengthening synapses and neural pathways. This ability to change is very important in the process of rewriting our stories and changing our perception of our world to see what's more helpful to us instead of what limits us.

During visualization, the brain is provided with images that it can store. Many professional organizations and athletes use this technique, just as Dr. Hamilton described, as additional practice for the brain to convert into memories. The brain, just like a computer, will scan its bank of data (memories) to recall something that will help in a specific moment.[89] For example, a golfer visualizes the correct form for their swing at times when physical practice is finished or not possible. Then, when playing in a tournament, the golfer recalls the proper swing technique, and the brain immediately scans for the memories of the real and visualized practice. The golfer executes it as it has been "practiced." This is literally game-changing for athletes, especially those who are recovering from an injury and don't want to lose valuable practice time.

Many successful companies use this technique before presentations to clients or in team-building exercises to reduce stress, improve confidence, and increase motivation. One of my employers uses mindset, mindfulness, and visualization to help employees provide better care to clients while not losing sight of their own emotional and physical health. My husband's company sends their employees to weeklong mindfulness and team-building workshops to teach them how to avoid burnout, be more client-oriented, and be better teammates and coworkers. The workshops focus on how to be a better version of oneself. The idea is that if you engage in adequate self-care, you'll be able to provide better care for your clients.

I'm currently working with a new mother who had a terrible relationship with her mother as a child. She never heard encouraging words, only how bad she was. She fears being like her mother while raising her children. She says that she hears words her mother used with her while she's interacting with her children. She wants to be a more patient and happier mother. We're working on refocusing on the idea that her past helped her realize what kind of parent she wants to be and, more importantly, that she knows firsthand what will not work. She knows how she doesn't want to raise her children. She uses visualization to change her mindset while interacting with her kids, picturing herself speaking kindly and calmly to her children and them smiling and laughing. She says that this helps her feel like a good mother and positive role model because it encourages her to stop and think before she speaks to them.

VISUALIZATION—A TWOFER (YOU KNOW, A TWO-FOR-ONE DEAL)

I once used this skill to help fix a problem without realizing it was solving two issues, a physical and a mental one. I was experiencing shin splints after running only short distances. After I was done with a training run, I would be shut down for days due to excruciating pain. I was training for my first ever real race, a 13.1-mile half-marathon, and I had only weeks until showtime. Not that I was expecting much, but I wanted to do my best. I was sad, angry, and frustrated that I couldn't figure out why this was happening. I knew what shin splints were, but I couldn't figure out why they were happening to me. I began to feel sorry for myself and mourned my situation a lot. I consulted doctors, physical therapists, and other professionals, and all of them told me that I needed to stop running. My friends and family told me to stop running since it caused me so much pain. I couldn't accept that this was the case. I was ready to give up, but my tenacity kicked in, and I refused to believe that I was done running. Running made me feel good. It helped me clear my head. It made me happy. I had so much I wanted to do and so many places I wanted to run.

I tried other things just to get through the race. The following week, I was purchasing compression braces for my shins and saw a flyer with the information for a professional running coach. This guy was a veritable guru of running. His qualifications for coaching were irrefutable. He was amazing. Surely, he could tell me what I was doing wrong or if my body was just screwed up and I'd never be able to run again. So, I called him, and we met at a local high school track. He watched me run and took pictures with a high-speed camera that showed every foot strike in slow motion. He asked me what kind of foot strike I ran with. This isn't something you teach yourself. It's just the way your brain tells your foot to hit the ground while running.

Some runners are heel planters, and the heel of their foot is what hits the ground first. Some are toe planters, and they run on their toes. Some are midfoot planters, and the middle part of their foot is the first to hit the ground. It doesn't really matter what way you plant unless it causes a problem. I thought for sure I had a midfoot plant. Well, my guru showed me frame by frame in slow motion how I ran.

And there it was—my heel hitting the ground first, sending thousands of pounds of pressure right up my shin. *Genius! He's a genius!* I thought. *That's what I'm doing wrong.* He figured me out. Then it hit me, *Shit! How do I fix this in a week?* He explained that there were drills I could do but that it usually takes some time to change the way you run. Of course it takes time to change your running form. This was how I had been running for, oh, *years*. Great! I didn't have time. I had two weeks. Shit, shit, shit, and more shit!

I had to do this fast. So, I learned the drills, practiced them, and got really serious about visualizing myself running with the middle of my foot striking the ground first. I imagined every day, many times a day—while I drank my coffee, while I ate my meals, and while I peed (because you really can't do anything else while you're peeing). What? It's a good use of time. I literally changed my running gait in days. This is very unusual, but I did it and ran the race *pain-free*, which was really all I expected to do. I owe my ability to finish my marathon to my guru, Richard, and to visualization. It worked for me. But I had no idea how well it could work for all things in life. At that time, I only knew about using the technique for sports. I was uninformed. I had yet to learn the true power of visualization.

I learned that visualization could help me be a better runner and be happier. While I visualized myself happily running, I was also creating power pathways. I was joyful again, and I did it through visualization without even realizing it. I was providing my brain with positive, happy thoughts every day. These happy thoughts, along with the mental images, formed a new pattern of thinking in my brain, which strengthened every time I activated the pathways by thinking about being happy. My brain was powerful. I was powerful. It was amazing. I was amazing!

Give your brain positive thoughts and imagined visions of you happy and succeeding. Do this repeatedly so that you activate the areas of the brain that can convert the thoughts into long-term memories and then into automatic thoughts.[90] Then your brain can help you achieve what you want to. When you tell your brain you can, it forms associations. The brain's ability to process information and then change and grow after learning something new, either from actual activity or visualization, involves the formation of new neurons (nerve cells), which create and strengthen new neural pathways for neurons to communicate. Therefore, the brain has the capacity to change problematic thinking and behavior into that which is more beneficial to us.[91] As we discussed earlier, this concept of neural plasticity is something anyone can use without special training, and the brain is very good at it.[92] I refer to this process as forming power pathways. But the opposite is true as well; the brain will be very good at forming or strengthening negative pathways if this is the information it receives. I refer to these as negative or weak pathways because they rob us of our strength and resiliency. We're not doing ourselves any favors by forming or strengthening this type of neural pathway. You can learn how to stop this, *but* don't expect to see a change if you don't make one.

CHAPTER 8

FAKE IT TILL YOU MAKE IT—MODELING

"The secret to change is to focus all of your energy,
not on fighting the old, but on building the new."[93]

—Dan Millman

The old expression "fake it till you make it" explains the technique of modeling. This isn't faking it at all; it's mimicking the behavior of someone who has been able to do what you want to do. Modeling is a very good way to learn what it takes to accomplish what you want, since you see someone else doing it and know it can be done. If you want to be a successful speaker, attend lectures from someone who speaks the way you want to. Do the things they do. If you see someone who's confident and you want to be like them, then be like them. Model their behavior. Hang around people who act the way you want to act. Watch them in action. Do what they do. If it can be done by someone else, then you can do it too. This is why athletes watch videos of other successful athletes. They study their technique, model it, and make it their own.

Winston Churchill, the World War II hero who helped lead the Allied forces to victory over Hitler, used to say, "I like things to happen, and if they don't happen, I like to make them happen."[94] My dad used to cite this quote, too. But I want you to know something about me. Even though I grew up hearing that quote, I thought I was mediocre at best—at everything! I had no real talents. I was a late bloomer and was more immature and younger than most of my classmates. I didn't like the way I looked and constantly compared myself to others. I wasn't kind to myself. I focused on things I didn't have instead of my qualities and, therefore, had no qualities because I never took the time to find them and nurture them. I was so worried about being compared to my peers that, at age eleven, I decided to "fake it" and play baseball with boys instead of softball with girls in our town's recreational league. That way, if I sucked, I could attribute it to being a girl on a boys' team. After all, boys should be better at baseball than me, or so I hoped everyone would believe.

As it turned out, I wasn't bad. I never let myself realize it then because my belief system was flawed, but I was better than all the boys on the team. I was even picked by my teammates for the all-star team. I thought this was because I was the only girl and they were being kind to me. You know, the token girl. At first, the boys were afraid to throw the ball to me since I was a girl. My coach yelled to them to quit hesitating and throw the ball because I could catch whatever they threw at me, and I did, no matter how hard the ball was thrown. I earned my spot as the team's first baseman for that reason. But somehow, I still thought my success was not my doing. I ended up hitting a lot of home runs. I remember my brother telling me that when he had asked what all the cheering was about, his friend replied, "It's just your sister. She hit another home run." Yet, despite everyone's acknowledgment, I still refused to allow myself to believe that I had talent. My belief system was flawed, *super* flawed.

The following year, sports were separated by gender, and I reluctantly tried softball at my parents' insistence. That didn't go so well for me. I had the talent, but I couldn't let myself believe it because, as everyone knows, baseball is easier than softball. At least that's what I told myself, so that became my reality. My belief system was, again, flawed. I never stopped to ask myself why I had such a negative bias.

Had I taken the time to realize that there was evidence to the contrary, I could have enjoyed the experience and possibly gone on to play in high school. But I continued with my flawed belief system and didn't realize until I was much older that I could, in fact, do whatever I wanted to do if I only believed I could. If Dr. Maltz were alive, he would tell me that since I believed I was a failure, I found situations to confirm this belief by finding ways to fail.[95] Believing that I could succeed was not consistent with my flawed belief system and, therefore, not possible.[96] I either didn't try because I knew I would fail or I didn't put my all into it because I didn't believe I could do it. Dr. Maltz was right; I found ways to fail. Damn! I wish I knew that back then.

I somehow managed to play soccer in high school. There were no tryouts, and everyone made the team. So, of course, in my mind, that's why they let me play. I just wanted to play. I had no expectations of being good because, in my mind, I wasn't good at anything. You can't be good if you don't think you can be. Looking back, I wasn't bad, but I never got better because I didn't think I could. This time, I let other things cloud my perception. More negative assumptions. I allowed myself to believe that others had the power to make me feel ashamed. I didn't yet know that I was the only person who could make me feel ashamed and that only I could control my emotions. It didn't occur to me that I was the problem and that my own assessment of myself was to blame.[97] My perspective was consistent with shame, and so I acted like someone who should be ashamed. I learned later in life that this self-assessment was incorrect. It was an opinion, my opinion, not the truth.

Through his extensive research and work providing care for people with deformities, Dr. Maltz found that our beliefs are based on our past accomplishments, mistakes, and experiences with others, and how we were treated. We create a mental picture of how we see ourselves, and this becomes our reality. He explains that "Once an idea or a belief about ourselves goes into this picture, it becomes 'true,' as far as we personally are concerned. We do not question its validity, but proceed to act upon it *just as if were true.*"⁹⁸ Problems occur when this mental picture is inaccurate. My mental picture was inaccurate as a child, and it carried into adulthood. I believed that I wasn't good enough at anything, and so that was my reality. I didn't question the validity of my beliefs, but lived my life as if they were indisputable. Not only did I believe I wasn't good at anything, I also let my family's financial situation define me as a person. Of course it didn't, but I let the shame of being poor further erode my self-esteem. I wish I hadn't done that.

SHAME

I grew up poor, really poor. My dad always said he would rather have the worst house on the best block than the best house on the worst block. His desire was for us to live in a safe neighborhood and attend a good school. Despite his inability to afford this, he eventually made it happen. I was ashamed of the house. I would take the sports bus home from soccer practice and get off three stops before my house so that no one could see me walking up to it. Mostly everyone on the bus knew where I lived, but I still couldn't listen to the comments made as I exited the bus in front of my house. The bus driver dropped everyone off at their houses, but I walked three extra blocks after grueling sprints at practice just to avoid potential judgment.

So, we had the worst house on a good block. It was on a nice little street in a safe town with a pretty good school system. I had two brothers and a sister, and we all lived in a two-bedroom house with a kitchen, living room, and one bathroom. I shared a bedroom with my three siblings until high school, when my dad was able to build an addition onto the house. It had a dirt porch for a long time, as the money for the renovations came in very slowly. But they finally came in and he finished the porch. He made it happen. He faked it until he made it.

My father was a good provider and protector of those he loved. You didn't mess with my dad. He was a small man, but everyone was afraid of him. He was an angry man, and I never knew why until my mother told me when I was older. He had a horrible childhood with no role model, even though he had four brothers, two sisters, and his mother and father. He could never please his father, who treated him like he wasn't worthy of his attention. In fact, my grandfather went out of his way to make sure my dad knew how little he meant to him. I found out the reason for this later in life.

A TERRIBLE, HORRIBLE THING

My dad was five years old when my grandparents left him in the car to watch their new baby boy while they did something they needed to do. He was told not to leave the car and to stay with the baby, who was lying on the back seat. But they took too long. My father became distracted, as five-year-olds often do, and the baby died. He rolled over and suffocated. This situation was wrong on so many levels, but none of it was the five-year-old's fault. Yet, he was blamed for something that no child should be responsible for, and the adults never forgave him. His siblings followed the adults and didn't question why the family treated him so harshly. It's possible this was due to the guilt his parents harbored for their negligence, but whatever the reason, my father didn't deserve that kind of punishment. A five-year-old little boy was placed in an impossible situation, and a tiny baby lost his life. There's no getting over that as a kid.

Dad continued to seek the approval of his family. When he didn't get it from them, he sought it in other ways. He wanted to be the expert that people turned to for advice and help with their construction issues. He would watch and listen to lawyers and construction experts in the courtroom. He modeled them. He learned from them and acted like them until he became an expert. He faked it until he made it. He would win cases in court as an expert witness on all matters of construction relating to the family business. His father and brothers could build what and where they planned to thanks to my dad. Lawyers would question him as to his schooling. He had no formal education, he didn't even graduate from high school, but he understood that he knew more than everyone in that courtroom, and he always prevailed. He read about and watched actual cases until he knew as much as the lawyers about construction law. He was so creative, and his brain worked like a computer. Despite this ability, his family never acknowledged his gift. They never thanked him or showed gratitude for their son's part in the success of the family business. They enjoyed wealth on the back of their son. He never got his fair share, yet he never wanted to alienate his family. He kept on solving their problems and making them money, but he never got what he deserved, ever.

PEARLS—PICK 'EM UP

I learned a lot from my dad. He was once paid a check by a client who he suspected was trying to swindle him. He tried to cash it and was informed that there were insufficient funds. Most people would have left angry and without their money. Not my dad. He asked the teller how much the account was short. When she asked why, he said he was considering putting a deposit into the account. She thought he was insane. "Make a deposit to someone else's account? You can't do that," she said. He calmly told her that he wasn't being deceitful or trying to steal anything and that this was a perfectly legal transaction. He explained that no one can take money from another person's account but that anyone can make a deposit to any account. It's not typical practice, but it is legal. She went to seek advice from her supervisor about this absurd request. When she returned, he asked how much the account was deficient. She stated that she couldn't give him that information because it was confidential. He further explained that he simply wanted to deposit the deficient amount so that he could cash his check and be on his way. He asked, "Is it more than two hundred dollars?" When she replied that it was not, he said, "Then I would like to make a deposit of two hundred dollars to this man's account." He did, and he was able to cash the check. It cost him $200 to get $9,800 of the $10,000 payment. He considered it a small price of doing business. Some people are shitty. He swindled the swindler.

My dad was a genius, or close to it. He was also very funny. He would share his wisdom in the form of humor. He would always say, "Dropping pearls here. You picking 'em up?" It was abundantly clear that he was the brains behind his family's construction business, but they would never admit that. They were resentful of his intelligence. He never doubted how smart he was. He didn't need anyone to tell him that. But he did spend most of his life seeking the approval of his family. He was in his fifties when he finally realized that he didn't need it. Despite this, he made sure he sent the message to us that we could do anything we wanted to do, and never let anyone tell us otherwise. I thought I understood this, but somehow, I missed that message. I didn't pick up that pearl.

What I missed was the realization that the loving and safe home I had was more important than what others said about it or me. I was too immature to realize that my dad was doing the best he could with what he had at the time. I later found out that he would have had so much more money if he had separated from the family business and gone out on his own. He was trying so hard to convince his family that he was good at what he did and that he could bring them success. He would find property, plan out what they could build on it, and bid the lowest price to get jobs. He always got the job, and they always made a lot of money because of this, but the split was never an even one. He was trying to make up for something that was never his fault, but they never forgave him.

I let the judgment of others cloud my view of what he was up against and what he gave up for his family. So did he. My mistake was trying to conceal what my life was like because I feared the judgment of others. My dad's mistake was believing that he had to prove himself to his family. His belief system was flawed. He thought, in order to be successful, he needed his family, but he was wrong. His family needed him to be successful. And although he knew this, he let his negative belief system get the better of him and talk him out of it. I let my belief system keep me from realizing any true potential I had. I was too busy hiding. Don't do that. Don't do what I or my dad did.

Pick something that you've always wanted to do, such as be more confident, and "fake it till you make it." Make things happen. This is a statement that people now laugh at and don't take seriously. But honestly, this statement is grounded in the psychiatric behavioral principle of modeling. In no way does it suggest that you fake being well when you're not. Nor does it suggest that you hide symptoms, which is masking them. That's not good.

Many people don't believe that this technique is helpful, and of course, there are *some* situations where it may not be, such as when I tried to fake that I was happy when I was not during my postpartum depression. I was masking my symptoms instead of getting treatment, making things worse. I needed medication. However, after starting the medication, I changed my attitude and helped myself mentally by using this principle.

Modeling is a technique widely used in group psychotherapy where new members learn by imitating or modeling the strengths and coping skills demonstrated by senior members in the group. This learning technique was studied and taught by Irvin Yalom, a pioneer whose work advanced the field of psychotherapy, especially in relation to group therapy.[99] The concept has evolved and is now used by professionals in almost every field who want to be better. Just ask a competitive athlete or CEO of a successful company how they use this technique.

The principle of not viewing oneself as a fraud, but rather as someone actively trying to develop a new habit, captures what my dad did. He didn't have a degree or education like those he encountered in his work, but he acted like he did, and he got the job done. He faked it until he made it happen, and I learned from him.

I wanted so badly to be a great runner but wasn't. I focused too much on how slow I was or how many miles I could run. I missed out on opportunities to enjoy something I wanted to do because I thought it was too complicated or I didn't have the natural talent needed to be great. Then, I met some super nice runners who encouraged me to join them on a run. I thought, *Shit. They're gonna leave me choking on their dust.* But then I thought, *So what if that happens?* So, I did. I decided to just jump in. I faked it. I pretended I was a good runner and told myself that I was and that I could run races with other runners who were way better than I was. I was mediocre at best, but I decided to get better. I hung out with more runners and joined their running group. It was made up of a bunch of runners who all had different levels of running fitness. Some were fast, some average, some slow, and some very slow. I had wasted my time worrying whether I could keep up. I fit in with the average runners (because you know, I was average . . . at everything). I realized how lucky I was to be running with a group of runners who accepted me and supported me on my running journey. It was beautiful. I was grateful. Why didn't I start this sooner? But that wasn't the end of it. Something great happened, something really amazing that I never dreamed I could do. More about this later.

CHAPTER 9

THE BOOMERANG
EFFECT OF KINDNESS

"Everything has beauty, but not everyone sees it."[100]

—*Confucius*

Pass around kindness like it's free money. Throw it out to all who will look or listen, and watch what comes right back at you. And while you're at it, be kind to yourself every day. Not only do you deserve it, but the universe needs kindness, and you won't be sorry if you do this. Say kind words to others randomly. Show kindness whenever the opportunity presents itself. You don't need to go out looking for it. You need only to open your eyes and notice everything. Opportunities are everywhere, right in front of you, and it costs nothing. You cannot lose by doing this. You can only gain. When someone shows you kindness, no matter how small an act, be grateful and pay it forward. Kindness thrown out to the universe changes lives—yours and those you extend it to. Don't pass by someone who drops something with their arms full, someone who needs help opening the door, someone in a rush who could use the spot you have in line, an elderly person who could use assistance, or anyone you see who could use a hand with something. Who knows what has happened to them recently? Who knows what they're going home to? Maybe today is the last straw that they can handle. Maybe you're making way more of a difference than you realize, and maybe they'll be forever grateful. We would all do well to take note of this quote by Lloyd

Shearer, "Resolve to be tender with the young, compassionate with the aged, sympathetic with the striving, and tolerant of the weak and the wrong. Sometime in life you will have been all of these."[101]

REDEFINING "KAREN"

Be a Karen! I know what you're thinking. You've seen that joke online: "Don't be a Karen!" Well, it's time to rethink that and extend some kindness to all the real Karens we know who are awesome and who are tired of hearing that joke. Let me explain. When I was eight years old, someone extended kindness to me in a big way. Her name was Karen, and I'll never forget her. I had a teacher in third grade whom we'll refer to as Mrs. O. I was unfortunate enough to have her again when she transferred to fifth grade. I was traumatized one day in reading group when everyone was laughing and I didn't know what the joke was. Turns out, my fly was down on my jeans. Now, this was no ordinary pair of jeans. They were high waisted, which meant the fly was very long. When the fly was down, the entire abdomen and underwear were visible, like a display in the window at Macy's. It was down that day. I was on display, and I was unaware. My teacher, the adult in the room, found it funny and laughed with the other children. Now, this didn't have to be the soul-shattering traumatic event that I believed it was. But it was. I allowed it to be. I was eight, and when you're eight and you look to an adult for help in diffusing a situation, and she is laughing at you, soul-crushing pretty much sums it up.

Only one student, Karen, was kind enough to get out of her seat, walk over to me, and whisper in my ear to inform me of the catastrophe that had unfolded. She was also eight years old but demonstrated more maturity than our teacher. I was devastated, and all Karen wanted to do was relieve my despair. I remember to this day how I felt when Mrs. O didn't help me but Karen did, even though she didn't have to. She could have done the easier thing and sit there, silently watching the show, enjoying a laugh. But it wasn't funny to her. I resolved from that day forward to extend kindness and show compassion to others whenever I had the opportunity, because I wanted others in times of need to feel the kindness Karen extended to me for no reason other than to be kind.

The same Karen felt so badly for a girl who wet her pants in seventh grade during lunch. Yes, seventh grade. Perhaps she had some issue that no one knew about. Maybe a urinary tract infection. Who knows what was going on in her life at that time? How absolutely mortified she must have felt. The poor girl was devastated and ran to the bathroom. Karen brought her lunch to her and ate it with her in the bathroom. The girl no doubt remembers how the room full of students laughed at her but also how Karen did whatever she could to relieve her distress. In the words of Mya Angelou, "I've learned that people will forget what you said, people will forget what you did, but people will never forget how you made them feel."[102] Karen made people feel cared about when others were unkind. Be a Karen whenever you can. It's easy.

LET'S NOT FORGET THE FOUR-LEGGEDS

This applies to animals as well. They are living, breathing creatures just like us, who feel fear and pain. They often just need a little help, and we should give it to them. Help a lost animal find its home. Put a baby bird back in the nest it fell out of. (Contrary to popular belief, birds cannot smell, and the mother will not reject its baby if you touch it, but she will appreciate the help since she has no way to do this on her own and the fallen babies become prey to other animals.) Call wildlife control for injured wild animals. Rescue a baby bunny that fell down a storm drain. Yes, this happens.

My brother Dan saw a baby rabbit fall down a storm drain and tried to remove the iron grate on the drain to get to it. A police officer came by and thought his actions were nefarious. He asked Dan to come over to the police cruiser. When Dan told the officer what he was doing, the officer looked surprised, and his attitude changed. He ran to his police car and came back with a tool. Dan was immediately relieved because let's just say that he's no stranger to the police. He's no criminal. In fact, he's a really good guy. But he's somehow always in the wrong place at the wrong time. So, the officer removed the grate. This is where it gets good, my favorite part of the story. I cried when my brother shared it with me because I'm a bleeding-heart animal lover. The officer held Dan's ankles while he went upside down into the drain to grab the bunny and bring it to safety. Thankfully, Dan's a little guy, or this may not have worked, but he would have figured out another way if it hadn't.

A little help is often the difference between life and death for animals. I'm not asking you to climb into a storm drain, but there are other things you can do. Make a call to animal control. Be kind. Save a life. It's easier than you think and very rewarding. Mahatma Gandhi reminds us that "The greatness of a nation and its moral progress can be judged by the way its animals are treated."[103] I love people who are kind to animals for many reasons, but mostly because they're usually even more kind to humans.

"IN A WORLD WHERE YOU CAN BE ANYTHING, BE KIND"
—Clare Pooley[104]

Be kind to animals. They know not cruelty, hate, negativity, jealousy, or greed. They can make even the hardest of hearts smile just by existing. Enjoy them. Sometimes they need a little help. So, help them. It costs you nothing but feels so good. Watch what happens in your life when you do. Pick up litter, cut soda can rings (animals get stuck in them), and help the environment. These selfless acts are easy, and they put you on a higher playing field of energy in life, above all the negativity. Living this way gives you purpose, extends your reach in the universe so that more is available to you, and cultivates happiness. Spreading kindness and gratitude has a boomerang effect. When you send them out, you receive them back. The only difference is that you receive way more than you gave. Don't believe me? Try it for a few weeks and see what happens.

GRATITUDE COMES IN MANY FORMS

About twenty years ago, I rescued a dog that had a hole in his head from a bullet. Yup! A bullet! In his head! Some people suck! He was a very sweet yellow Lab/mixed-breed dog who was in obvious discomfort, yet showed no aggression at all. As a member of the local volunteer humane society (comprised of myself and a small group of other women), I took him to the veterinary clinic in the rural area where he was found. They cleaned up his wound and commented on what a sweet, loving dog he was. There was no way I was going to send him to the shelter to be euthanized if no one adopted him. He was found with no collar, which meant he had one week to be adopted. I now keep collars of all sizes in my car so that when I find a stray, I can pop one on and buy them more time to live and possibly find a home. I wanted to adopt him and show him what kindness was, but I needed to focus on finding placements, since there would always be another and another in need of a loving home. The humane society, with the money they raised, paid for him to stay at the clinic while we found him a home worthy of his gentle, loving disposition. I was so pleased with the family that adopted him. It was a couple with a young daughter with special needs. She was about five years old. They thought they were adopting a sweet family pet, but they were so wrong. He was so much more.

This dog turned out to be no ordinary dog. He helped a little girl with special needs learn to calm herself. He sensed her anxiety whenever she would start to become agitated and worked his canine magic to relieve her worry. He did this without special training. It was just his natural-born talent and desire to protect those he loved. The family sent me a picture with a letter of gratitude for rescuing him and finding them to be his new family. *They* thanked *me!* Yet, I am forever grateful to them and to the Humane Society of Pulaski County in Virginia for allowing me to help this little girl live an easier, happier life and, of course, give Ben a second chance at life. Gentle Ben—great friend, natural service animal, and loving family member.

This story is not about a dog rescue. It's about five lives that were forever changed on one day—a little girl; her parents; a woman with a passion for helping; and an injured, homeless dog. All of them were eternally grateful for each other. Beautiful.

Be grateful for every little thing in your life that is good. Celebrate the wins no matter how small. Make a big deal of them. Don't run through life missing out on opportunities to appreciate whatever happiness comes your way. Stop and smell the roses. That's a real technique that most likely came from someone practicing mindfulness, not just some silly cliché that people say. Make the choice to be grateful. You can start right now. Think of a kind act that was done for you or even one that you witnessed someone else doing. Think of how good it made you feel, and then think of it again. Once you start doing this, you will be changed. You will experience life as you never have before. If you routinely show others kindness, thank you. I appreciate you and so does the universe. How do I know this? Because my boomerang comes back to me on a weekly basis. I don't let a beautiful day get away from me. I make a point to enjoy it and point it out to others.

CHAPTER 10

THE CHOICE

"One day or day one. You decide."[105]

—*Floriana NK*

Do yourself a favor: decide to lose sight of the things you lack. The most important decision you can make in your life is the decision to be happy. It is a choice. You can choose to wallow in your unhappiness and focus all your energy on what's wrong, but doing this is not helpful to you. Trust me, it doesn't work. It will rob you of enjoying everything beautiful that's right in front of you. It's a choice to find happiness, focus on it, and continue to fixate on it by noticing things that make you happy instead of rushing through your days without taking note of the beauty life has to offer. We are human, so we will, at times, become sad, irritable, or angry and focus on what's happening in that moment. That's OK, and it's normal. We need to accept that we feel how we feel and not judge ourselves harshly or feel guilty. But redirecting our focus to more useful things can lift us out of the negative emotions. Sound sappy? Maybe, but it's irrefutable. Remember the Harvard study on happiness? The longest-running study ever performed consistently confirms this. The participants in the study chose to focus on the people who love them and on being happy with them, which perpetuated feelings of happiness.[106]

Focusing on the problems in your life makes them more of a problem. This keeps you down, in the dark, and limited. It prevents the light from entering because you're too focused on the dark to make room for it. This mindset perpetuates the cycle of unhappiness, sadness, and negativity, which prevents the brain from forming neural pathways that can help you operate from a position of power. We all know a Debbie Downer. They speak constantly of their problems, the severity of which usually increases as they talk about them. They can always top your grief. Things just never go right for them, and it's no surprise why this happens. Good things don't happen when you only expect bad things. Start expecting good things to happen even if you don't know what they are yet. I bet you can think of some. Be open to them. Decide to develop power pathways instead of negative pathways. You have the power to do this. Use it. Choose to be powerful.

How do you do this? Notice everything that makes you smile. Do this every day. If you don't see anything, then think of past happy events repeatedly so that the good things stand out in your brain and are easy to recall. When you decide to be happy and focus your attention on things that make you feel that way, you bombard your brain with positive thoughts and images and allow it to convert these images into long-term memories.

When I was suffering from postpartum depression in what I refer to as my "dark years," my focus was on negative things. I was able to finally see the light when I realized that what was right in front of me was something to be happy for, proud of, and fortunate to have. This was my family—my parents, siblings, husband, and three children. I was not alone. I had people I loved who loved me.

I had glimpses of happy moments when my children would make me smile, but they were short-lived. Why? They were with me every day. So, why couldn't I notice these things every day? I started focusing on what was right in front of me. This is what ultimately lifted the darkness and revealed the light. Once I changed my focus and made it a habit to refocus when things didn't go as expected, I was able to find my strength and resilience. Remember the words of

Abraham Lincoln: "Folks are usually about as happy as they make up their minds to be."[107] Make up your mind to be happy, right now. If you have difficulty finding happy situations because you've only noticed the negative for so long, then create a few in your mind. Imagine yourself in happy places, in happy situations, and doing happy things that make you feel good. Remember the Lerner study discussed earlier? The one that demonstrated how the brain doesn't know the difference between seeing or experiencing and imagining? Imagining what you want your life to be is a very powerful tool in your toolbox, and it is available to you right now.

Remind yourself of your strengths. We all have them. If you don't know what they are, ask someone close to you. They know. If you're good at a sport, remind yourself of times when you played well. If you're good at art, remind yourself of your best work. If you're good at solving problems, remind yourself of the times you helped someone with their problem. Tell yourself you're a great person, spouse, sibling, friend, coworker, employee, neighbor, etcetera. Recall these moments and allow your brain to experience them again and again. Visualize them every day, several times a day, until they become automatic thoughts. These are the thoughts we want to get stuck. Repetition is the world's best teacher. That's where your power is. That's where your brain can really help you. The more you hear and do these things, the stronger the positive thoughts become until they form a power pathway. (You're welcome for the power pathway you're forming while rereading important concepts in this book.) While you're doing this, be kind to yourself. You deserve it.

Tell yourself that you intend to be happy and repeat it often. Talk to yourself kindly. Let yourself appreciate that "you got this" and use uplifting messages. Put sticky notes on your computer screen with thoughtful messages to yourself about things you have accomplished or intend to accomplish. Be specific. Then, believe it. You *must* believe it. Remind yourself when you accomplish something and think about how you did it. If you're doing something difficult, visualize yourself completing it. Imagine the completed task and allow your brain to see yourself happy with the finished product. Don't be concerned that it's not yet finished. Visualize it anyway. Remember the Harvard study with the piano players? The brain doesn't discriminate between something you did and something that you imagined you did. Don't believe it? Just ask an athlete. This concept is so well studied and documented that colleges and high schools teach their athletes to use it. It's used by professional athletes, CEOs, speakers, writers, artists, and surgeons. The list is exhaustive. Anyone can use this technique for anything they want to do.

BE THE BEAM

My daughter competed on a United States of America Gymnastics team. She was the "beam queen" for a long time, but in high school she developed a "block," as gymnasts refer to it. She couldn't complete some of the tricks she had previously mastered and successfully landed on the balance beam hundreds of times or more. We discussed this at length. I discovered that while on the beam just before beginning a trick, she was telling herself *Don't fall* over and over. That was the reason for her inability to perform. She was essentially instructing her brain to fall even though that wasn't her intention. Using negative terminology creates a negative thought that gets stuck in the brain and then becomes reality. The brain focuses on the word *fall*, and since the brain is the mother of all organs, the body obeys. She changed her thoughts to *Stay on the beam* and *Stick it*, which were positive and helpful. Actually, it morphed into *Be the beam, Cass*, as some of her friends would yell this to her, cheering her on and reminding her to keep a positive mindset just before mounting the beam. This phrase "stuck," thankfully, and these helpful thoughts sent her brain positive messages, making positive outcomes more likely.

Your words are important. So, watch what you say. Your thoughts are important. So, watch what you think! My daughter was able to use positive thoughts and self-talk along with visualizing herself landing the trick to overcome her mental block. The beam queen was back! She had thought herself right back into her reign.

Choose to be grateful for yourself, your life, and those who matter to you. Appreciate all that you have, all that you are, and all that you have yet to become. Give yourself a break when you're hard on yourself. So often we extend grace to others for hurting our feelings or mistakenly wronging us. This is OK. It's good to forgive. Our response is that we understand or that it's OK because someone was having a bad day. But what isn't OK is that we beat ourselves up if we accidentally do the same to someone else. We don't give that same grace to ourselves. We ruminate about what we should or shouldn't have done or said and worry ourselves right down the rabbit hole. Don't fall into this hole. Stop the worry in its tracks before it spirals. It doesn't matter what someone else thinks of what you said or didn't say. Worrying about something that hasn't happened and may never happen is a waste of your precious time—time that could be spent thinking of things that will help you rather than things that will make you feel worse.

I know what you're saying right now. If you could stop that cycle, you would have done so already and wouldn't need my help. Although it isn't difficult to change, you may need some guidance.

Choose to realize that there is another perspective of what you're worrying about. As discussed in chapter 3, what-if thinking isn't good for us. Unhelpful what-if thinking essentially creates things to worry about. These things haven't happened and may never happen. However, questioning can be a great thing if it revolves around the possibilities that life holds for us. Potential job opportunities, things we aspire to achieve, and other positive what-ifs are good examples of this. We need to convince our brain that there are other things to focus on. Change your what-if thinking from what could go wrong to what if your statements were taken in the best context. What if the statement wasn't even impactful at all and you have nothing to worry about?

Choose to uplift instead of criticize. Be a Karen. Not the Karen you're thinking of. The Karen you read about earlier. This applies to yourself as well as others. Choose to believe what you know instead of what others say. Just because they say it doesn't make it so. As Derek Jeter, team captain of the New York Yankees, arguably the best clutch hitter ever to play baseball, and all-around beautiful person, said, "Sometimes people complicate things by thinking too much about what someone might think of what they said or did."[108] He chose to lead his team with class and encouragement straight to the World Series. He focused on what could be improved, not what they did wrong. He never said an unkind thing about anyone, even when the media coaxed him to do so. It's possible that one of the things that helped him stay positive was that he paid no attention to what others said about him unless it deserved a thank you. He did his own thing and became very successful. He focused on what was going well in his life and was grateful for those who lifted him up in the process, especially his parents. He thanks them in his books for their encouragement and support. And you know what else he did? He became a role model for children, teenagers, athletes, and people in general. He reminds us that "Your image isn't your character. Character is what you are as a person."[109] What you are as a person is what you decide to be, and what you decide to be is a choice!

CHAPTER II

PUTTING IT ALL TOGETHER— YOUR TOOLBOX

"A good tool improves the way you work. A great tool improves the way you think."[110]

—*Jeff Duntemann*

To cultivate your own happiness, you will use everything in your toolbox just like a builder does to construct a house. Builders have their favorite tools, and you will too. You will build your own happiness and create your own opportunities, which can look however you wish.

In the previous chapters, we discussed some of the main tools that you can choose from to complete your toolbox. This chapter recaps what was already discussed in a list format for you to refer to and provides some other examples of how these techniques can work. If something doesn't work for you, you can take it out of your mental toolbox. If something works really well, you can use it over and over. It can be your go-to tool. You can even combine the techniques to match your needs and pull them out when needed.

LET'S RECAP OUR TOOLS—THE *T* OF THE PAT METHOD

Therapy and medication are tools you can use. You should seek the help of a professional to start if you feel you're unable to get unstuck without them. You could begin with therapy for support in understanding what you're feeling. Therapists can help you learn coping techniques and see if medication may be necessary. If it is, they can refer you to someone who can prescribe it. The prescriber will discuss your symptoms, and clarify if medication is indicated, and then discuss the choices, side effects, risks, and benefits to medication. You can also inquire about whether your symptoms can be improved with the use of noninvasive treatments like TMS. Together, you'll come up with a collaborative plan to treat your symptoms. You're in charge in this situation. You must be comfortable with the plan, and if you're not, seek clarification or an alternate plan. There's never only one choice. In addition, or if medication isn't indicated, you can use your toolbox of techniques to address what you're feeling.

Deep grounding breaths—Always, always, always use your grounding breaths for any circumstance where you feel unsettled, anxious, stressed, or in need of grounding. Do this whenever you feel as if a spiral is imminent or even just to feel calmer for no particular reason. Have your feet firmly planted on the ground. Close your eyes. Take a slow, deep breath in to the count of four while visualizing the air filling your lungs, and then expel it while seeing it leave your lungs, taking with it any anxiety, stress, or anger. Then, before the next one, tell yourself that you are calm and that you are calming yourself because you can do so. Repeat this activity at least three times, or more if necessary.

Cognitive restructuring (assess the damage)—Change your thoughts. See a different perspective of what's going on. Assess the damage. Ask yourself if the situation is really as bad as you think. What is the consequence? Will it matter one week, one month, or one year from now? If not, then forget it! Let it go. Instead, focus your energy on what's going well for you. Tell yourself that things happen to everyone and not everything is worthy of your energy. Don't create catastrophes out of insignificant events. If you said something or acted in a way that you worry will cause you embarrassment, don't dwell on it. Don't worry about something that you can't be sure will even happen. Know that others don't think about you or what you say or do in that kind of detail. They're most likely not dwelling on it. Release it to the universe and move on to what is good.

Mindfulness, positive self-talk, and mantras—Use these multiple times a day, every day. Allow yourself to appreciate the small things (as well as the big things) that happen in your everyday life. Don't pass up a moment to feel the pleasure they bring. Bombard your brain with positive thoughts. Say them out loud so that you stimulate more senses. Say them, hear them, and even write them. The more senses we activate, the easier it is to remember the thought and then to recall it when we need it. We want these good thoughts to get stuck so there's no room for negative thoughts. Spread positive words to others. When we actively speak positively, we get positivity back from others. This will also serve another purpose: to decrease the stigma of mental health, which benefits everyone.

Modeling (fake it till you make it)—If you want to be better at something, find someone who does it well and model them. Act like them. Behave as if you are what you want to be. Fake it until you make it. Your actions will follow your thoughts, so believe that you can be better at what you want to excel at.

Visualization—See positive mental images in your mind as if you're looking at them in real life. Make them detailed and remember them often. We want these images and thoughts to become stuck so that we can recall them automatically. They will push the bad images and thoughts out of the memory bank. They will replace the negative images and soon become your go-to visuals.

Journaling—Keep a journal of the things that went well and made you feel good. If things go wrong, don't focus on their wrongness but on what you will do to fix them. Focus on the solution. Find at least one good thing about the day and write it down. If you have racing thoughts you cannot stop thinking about, write these down and then shred them.

Meditation and guided imagery—Take whatever time you can spare and go to a quiet place to think of things that make you feel calm. Visualize yourself in the calmest of settings and note yourself looking, feeling, and acting calmly. Breathe deeply while you do this to remove any negative energy you're harboring. Remember that there are also guided meditation apps where you follow along with a coach who directs you. Some people like this type of meditation, as they don't have to think of what to do.

Good enough—Don't try to be perfect. As Dr. Maxwell Maltz and Dr. Donald Winnicott have shared, this is counterproductive. They say that perfection robs us of enjoying anything because we're always unhappy with what we did and want it to be better.[iii] Know that good enough is often better, and appreciate the small wins while you're at it.

Believe—Most important of all is that you must believe that you can get unstuck and have the life you want. Belief in yourself is paramount for success in life.

RED HILL

My dad would always tell my siblings and me to "unlearn the word can't; remove it from your vocabulary completely!" He followed his own advice on this. However, he passed away before he realized his superpower. He struggled most of his life to provide for his family, but he never let anyone tell him he couldn't do something. He would say, "How do they know?" "Who are they?" and, best of all, "They don't know me or what I can do." He started out without a nickel to his name. He had a horrible childhood and parents he couldn't possibly please but continued to try. He let what they told him he was hold him down. He was a struggling property developer. He had a vision to buy a piece of land in our neighborhood in West Long Branch, New Jersey, that all the kids called "Red Hill" because it was a huge hill of reddish-colored dirt with a sandlot at the base of it bigger than a baseball field. It was fun to play on as a kid, but it was a big eyesore to the town. Most developers believed it wasn't worth the effort or couldn't figure out a way to build on it. My dad figured out a way. He believed that he could do it.

Everyone told him he couldn't develop it, including his developer father and brothers. "Can't be done," they told my dad. He knew it could be but didn't have the money to buy the land. He didn't let that stop him. He was so creative that he told the man who owned it that he would have the money in a week and to *not* sell it to anyone else. So, the deal was sealed with a handshake. My dad was a man of his word and was known for that. He was one of the smartest and most honest men I've ever met.

So, Dad came up with a plan to make it happen. It was a creative plan and one that arguably no other developer had the talent or guts to try. He sold the dirt on the land that he didn't yet own to pay the man who owned the land. My brother and I counted loads of dirt as they left Red Hill in dump trucks. My dad used the money he earned for those loads of dirt to pay for the land that he later developed into a nice residential development he named Primrose Lane. This was genius. He did something that everyone else believed they couldn't because they let someone else tell them that it wasn't possible. It wasn't a dishonest move. The two men made a deal, and it was honored. The land was Dad's if he came up with the money in one week as he promised, and he did. There were no rules as to how he did this. There were no contractual details or legalese. He saw no difference; sell the dirt after you pay for the land or sell the dirt and then pay for the land—chicken or the egg. He knew it could be done, and he did it despite the obstacles. Both men were happy. My dad saw the opportunity in the difficulty instead of the difficulty in the opportunity. He proved the others wrong. He made things happen because he believed he could.

CHAPTER 12

FIND YOUR SUPERPOWER

"Whatever the mind of man can conceive and
believe, it can achieve."[112]

—*Napoleon Hill*

It's true; your superpower, the way to get unstuck, is right in front of you. It's always available to you. Now that you have learned the tools, you can complete your toolbox. You can start using these tactics this very minute. If you still have doubts, hang with me on this for some powerful proof. Believe you can do what you want. Happiness starts as a habit and becomes a lifestyle. It's a choice. I made a choice to be happy and to do something that I never thought I could because I was holding onto my limiting beliefs. Life became great because I let go of those beliefs and changed my perception of myself from someone who could not to someone who could. I rewrote my story and then watched it unfold. And as my new story unfolded, I did something I thought was amazing.

Believe you can change your future. I did. Your past doesn't determine your future in any way. Mine didn't. Use what tools you have learned, and allow yourself to view your experience in a different way. Release the chains that keep you tied to unhappiness. Free yourself to experience what matters in life. Allow yourself to be happy. Anything is possible, even for mediocre runners like me. Don't believe me? Check this out.

THE BRAIN IS THE BOSS (AND THE BODY IS A KIND OF ASSISTANT MANAGER)

I wanted to be a better runner, so I ran more. I got better, but I was lacking something. I was missing the belief that I could do amazing things. Every runner wants to place in the top three in their age group in a race. I wished I could, but I believed that my body couldn't possibly place in the top three in a race because I was only an average runner, and average runners never place. This was a limiting belief. It limited me for most of my life. If I had continued to think this way, I never would have progressed. I had average speed and was able to run an average distance but decided I wanted to be a great runner. Get that? I *decided* to be a better runner. So, I started running with a group of ultra runners who were significantly better than I was.

Ultrarunning involves running distances greater than marathon distance, which is 26.2 miles. I visualized myself running and crossing the finish line in an ultramarathon. I spoke to myself in encouraging ways while I ran and while not running. I sought the advice of accomplished runners and really listened to them. I ate what they ate, drank what they drank, wore what they wore, read what they suggested, acted like them, and followed every piece of advice they provided. When I ran, I allowed myself to enjoy my environment and everything I saw while running. I noticed everything. My speed got faster—not much, but a bit. Hey, progress is progress. The little things matter soooo much! I told myself that I was fast and that I had stamina for longer distances. I had failures, but I refused to view them as such. They were part of the journey, and they helped me realize what I did wrong that I could change next time, like eating more carbs, using different running shoes, changing sweaty clothes on long runs, and resting more in between training runs. But most importantly, I believed I was getting better. I continued visualizing myself running, but then I got more specific. I wanted more. So, I visualized bigger wins. Now, remember, I had never won or even placed in a race . . . ever. I wanted to but thought that was out of sight for me, above my ability level, because I was an average runner.

I began to change my belief system. What if I wasn't average? What if I was better than average? I wondered how many miles I could run before dropping. Not something average runners think of, or even something normal people think of. But maybe I wasn't normal. I didn't know. I did know that I didn't have a self-imposed cap regarding my mileage, no wall that I had to stop at once I reached it. What if I could run a fifty-mile race and just cross the line? Even if I was in last place, I would still cross, still accomplish it.

So, I got really serious, changed my perspective, and did something scary. I impulsively signed up for a fifty-mile race. Me! A fifty-mile race! Holy shit! I panicked. I hadn't improved my running enough to do a race of that caliber, but I wanted it and would never know if I could do it if I didn't try it. So I tried.

Not only did I hit my goal of fifty miles, I surpassed it and did sixty-five miles. That was such a huge confidence booster, and although it was difficult, I wanted more. So, I allowed myself to feel proud of my accomplishment and tried for more. I found out that some people actually run one hundred miles. I couldn't even imagine this, but suddenly I wanted to run one hundred miles! I signed up for a one-hundred-mile ultramarathon—the holy grail of ultrarunning. Then, I panicked again because this was real. Real stupid. It was hard enough to do fifty, and I had just committed to one hundred. Then I got out of my own way and started a training plan.

I had great days and bad days—days when I felt like Wonder Woman herself and other days when I wondered how I ever learned to walk. I didn't let the bad days defeat me. I let them show me that I needed to change something or simply suck it up and realize that I'm human. Every run cannot be a great run. But I managed to stay on my feet, mostly—except when I didn't. I ate dirt once or twice, but all runners do. I tried to laugh and let others laugh at me, because my scraped-up face, hands, and knees were kind of funny. Besides, I felt tough.

SHOWTIME

Then, race day came, and I got lost on the way to the event, which was more than an hour from my home. I was thirty minutes late and missed the start. I started to panic, and my brain began to spiral for a hot minute. My dream was shot before it started. But then I realized I wasn't running a timed race; I was running for mileage. I had a time frame in mind, but ultrarunning is more about mileage. So, I grounded myself and started my race at my time and my pace.

Then, something amazing happened. I looked at the leaderboard and I was in sixth place. I was so excited until I realized that I hadn't even completed thirty miles yet and that placement meant nothing so early on. But it felt great to see anyway, and I needed to feel great about something. Then something more amazing happened. I started climbing up in rank. Me, the average runner, was in fifth place after fifty miles. After that, I didn't care where I was on the leaderboard. I wanted only to get to one hundred miles, and then I would stop. About twenty hours later, I hit one hundred miles and cracked a bottle of champagne that another runner who was running fifty miles had brought with her. I waddled to my car, tired, cold, and cramped and went to sleep for two hours until daylight.

When I woke, I was so pleased with myself. I then went to hang out with the runner who had shared her champagne with me. I just love runners. I've never met one I didn't like. We pump each other up. She asked me why I stopped running. I informed her that I had planned to run one hundred miles, and I did one hundred miles. I was ready for breakfast and the award ceremony, which I was definitely not going to be in. She informed me that I still had time to run more before the race closed and the awards began. Actually, what she said was "Don't be stupid. You have more time. Get out there!" I had no intention of doing more than one hundred miles. I never dreamed that I would place. She told me that I was in fourth place and that I was crazy to stop there. She practically pushed me to the course. So, I started again and got about two and a half more miles before another runner told me that I had better hurry up because time was just about up. The race was ending, and I was only halfway finished with the last mile, which wouldn't be counted if I didn't cross the finish.

There was no way I was going to run a mile that didn't count. So, I ran my fastest mile in my last mile just to put it on the board. I could hardly breathe, but I crossed. That was crazy. A young woman walked past me and said she had been tracking my race all night and was so happy when I stopped running because she was in third place. *Great!* I thought. She was sweet. She deserved it. I congratulated her and tried to find a seat before I fell over, but she was still standing in my way. She so nicely informed me that she was disappointed when I started again because I knocked her from third place. I turned to see who she was speaking to because I was certain it wasn't me. But it was. I apologized to her, and she congratulated me. I hugged her and ran to the leaderboard, and sure enough, it was me in third place. Me!!

I, the average runner, placed third in an international ultramarathon with a total mileage of 103 in forty hours. I had wanted to find out what number of miles I would drop at. Turns out I still don't know because it wasn't 103! I was still standing and walking. In fact, I jumped and skipped around like a child. I had found my superpower. Maybe you can guess what it is. Nope, not running. It's will and a bunch of tenacity. I refused to give up.

As the famous proverb goes, "Where there's a will, there's a way." But my dad added "and you, my dear, have plenty of will." He was right.

I accomplished my dream not because I was amazing but because I believed I could! See, if we change our belief system from "I can't," which prevents us from even trying, to "I believe I can," we open up our world to amazing things we may never have had the opportunity to experience otherwise simply because we never thought we could. Add some gratitude, visualization, positive self-talk, modeling, and other behavioral tools and watch what *else* can happen. I changed my negative pathways to power pathways by telling myself I could. My brain became powerful and helped me become powerful.

I have since reunited with my husband and we're planning to remarry. I have more in store for myself. I continue to refocus my thoughts on what I can do using the PAT method, as I have found my *H*, my happiness, along my PATH. I turned the PAT method into my PATH to fulfillment in my life.

Congratulations, you have learned how to use the PAT method. Go forth and find your *H*, your PATH to happiness. While on the journey, be grateful for you, everything you have to offer the universe, and all the universe has to offer you. End your unhappiness. Start on your PATH to happiness and fulfillment right now. You can do it!

"The End is Where We Start From"
—T.S. Eliot

RECOMMENDED READING:

The Power of Intention by Dr. Wayne Dyer

Psycho-Cybernetics by Dr. Maxwell Maltz

The *Badass* series by Jen Sincero

How Bad Do You Want It by Matt Fitzgerald

The Obstacle is the Way by Ryan Holiday

Can't Hurt Me by Davis Goggins

The Feel Good Effect by Robyn Conley Downs

ACKNOWLEDGMENTS

I would like to thank:

My clients for their trust in me to be a part of their journey to wellness and happiness, and for allowing me to share their experiences with the hope that it will help others get unstuck.

My partners Valerie Magrino, Olga Esterov, and Marla Jensen at Shrewsbury Wellness Center—where so much goodness happens—for their mentorship, guidance, support, and friendship, and for their sincere interest in my success.

My editing and publishing team, Ashley Mansour, Rachel Warmath, Feli Arrieta, Chelsea Morning, and Jessica Reino, for their guidance and commitment to my success as an author.

Dr. Sahar M. Shafey for encouraging me—no, insisting that I become a psychiatric nurse practitioner. I am forever grateful for your faith in me and for your guidance.

I am eternally grateful and honored to know you all.

ENDNOTES

1   Maxwell Maltz, Psycho-Cybernetics, Updated and Expanded ed. (New York: TarcherPerigee, 2015), 74

2   Amrisha Vaish, Tobias Grossmann, and Amanda Woodward, "Not All Emotions Are Created Equal: The Negativity Bias in Social-Emotional Development," Psychological Bulletin 134, no. 3 (May 2008): 383, https://doi.org/10.1037/0033-2909.134.3.383.

3   Vaish, Grossmann, and Woodward, "Not All Emotions Are Created Equal," 383.

4   Vaish, Grossmann, and Woodward, "Not All Emotions Are Created Equal," 391.

5   Maltz, Psycho-Cybernetics, 4-5, 84-5.

6   Benjamin James Sadock, Virginia Alcott Sadock, and Pedro Ruiz, Synopsis of Psychiatry, 11th ed. (Philadelphia: Wolters Kluwer, 2015), 188, 190.

7   "Meditations Quotes," Goodreads, accessed May 13, 2024, www.goodreads.com/work/quotes/31010.

8   "When You've Exhausted All Possibilities, Remember This: You Haven't!" Quote Investigator, October 21, 2022, https://quoteinvestigator.com/2022/10/21/exhausted/.

9   American Psychiatric Association, The Diagnostic and Statistical Manual of Mental Disorders, 5th ed. (Arlington, TX: American Psychiatric Publishing, 2013), 160-1.

10 "Folks Are Usually about as Happy as They Make Up Their Minds to Be," Quote Investigator, October 20, 2012, https://quoteinvestigator.com/2012/10/20/happy-minds/#google_vignette.

11   American Psychiatric Association, The Diagnostic and Statistical Manual of Mental Disorders, 238-9.

12   Sally M. Winston and Martin N. Seif, Overcoming Unwanted Intrusive Thoughts: A CBT-Based Guide to Getting Over Frightening, Obsessive, or Disturbing Thoughts (Oakland, CA: New Harbinger Publications, 2017), 10.

13   Maltz, Psycho-Cybernetics.

14   Maltz, Psycho-Cybernetics, 148.

15   "We Cannot Go Back and Start Over, But We Can Begin Now, and Make a New Ending," Quote Investigator, November 5, 2015, https://quoteinvestigator.com/2015/11/05/new-ending/#:~:text=You%20can't%20go%20back,and%20someone%20named%20Carl%20Bard.

16   Maltz, Psycho-Cybernetics, 129.

17   Maltz, Psycho-Cybernetics, 14.

18   Napoleon Hill, Think and Grow Rich (Meriden, CT: The Ralston Society, 1937).

19   Maltz, Psycho-Cybernetics, 52.

20   Robert Waldinger, "Author Talks: The World's Longest Study of Adult Development Finds the Key to Happy Living," interview by Molly Liebergall, McKinsey & Company, February 16, 2023, https://www.mckinsey.com/featured-insights/mckinsey-on-books/author-talks-the-worlds-longest-study-of-adult-development-finds-the-key-to-happy-living#/.

21   Maltz, Psycho-Cybernetics, 113.

22   Maltz, Psycho-Cybernetics, 2.

23   Maltz, Psycho-Cybernetics, 52.

24 Maltz, Psycho-Cybernetics, 261-264.

25 Joachim Krausse and Claude Lichtenstein, eds. Your Private Sky: Discourse—R. Buckminster Fuller (Zürich: Lars Müller Publishers, 2001), 17.

26 "What We Call the Beginning is Often the End," BrainyQuote, accessed May 13, 2024, https://www.brainyquote.com/quotes/t_s_eliot_101421.

27 "Whether You Believe You Can Do a Thing or Not, You Are Right," Quote Investigator, February 3, 2015, https://quoteinvestigator.com/2015/02/03/you-can/.

28 "How Fast Can Neurons Transmit Through Your Body for the Nervous System to Function?" UCSB ScienceLine, October 25, 2016, http://scienceline.ucsb.edu/getkey.php?key=5607.

29 Winston and Seif, Overcoming Unwanted Intrusive Thoughts, 95.

30 Jodie A. Trafton, William P. Gordon, and Supriya Misra, Training Your Brain to Adopt Healthful Habits: Mastering the Five Brain Challenges, 3rd ed. (Los Altos, CA: Institute for Brain Potential, 2019), 139.

31 Trafton, Gordon, and Misra, Training Your Brain to Adopt Healthful Habits, 250.

32 Winston and Seif, Overcoming Unwanted Intrusive Thoughts, 89; Trafton, Gordon, and Misra, Training Your Brain to Adopt Healthful Habits.

33 Sadock, Sadock, and Ruiz, Synopsis of Psychiatry.

34 "If You Realized How Powerful Your Thoughts Are, You Would Never Think a Negative Thought," BrainyQuote, accessed May 14, 2024, https://www.brainyquote.com/quotes/peace_pilgrim_183377#:~:text=Peace%20Pilgrim%20Quotes&text=If%20you%20realized%20how%20powerful%20your%20thoughts%20are%2C%20you,never%20think%20a%20negative%20thought.

35   Maltz, Psycho-Cybernetics, 220.

36   Sadock, Sadock, and Ruiz, Synopsis of Psychiatry.

37   Maltz, Psycho-Cybernetics, 56.

38   Sadock, Sadock, and Ruiz, Synopsis of Psychiatry.

39   Martin E. P. Seligman, Learned Optimism: How to Change Your Mind and Your Life (New York: Vintage Books, 2006).

40   Jeremy Sutton, "Martin Seligman's Positive Psychology Theory," Positive Psychology, October 4, 2016, https://positivepsychology.com/positive-psychology-theory/.

41   Sutton, "Martin Seligman's Positive Psychology Theory."

42   Sutton, "Martin Seligman's Positive Psychology Theory."

43   Maltz, Psycho-Cybernetics, 109.

44   Maltz, Psycho-Cybernetics.

45   Sutton, "Martin Seligman's Positive Psychology Theory."

46   Dan Millman, The Way of the Peaceful Warrior (Tiburon, CA: HJ Kramer, 2000).

47   "Medicine Is Not Only a Science; It Is Also an Art. It Does Not Consist of Compounding Pills and Plasters; It Deals with the Very Processes of Life, Which Must Be Understood before They May Be Guided," BrainyQuote, accessed May 13, 2024, https://www.brainyquote.com/quotes/paracelsus_170321.

48   "The First Step Towards Getting Somewhere is to Decide You're Not Going to Stay Where You Are," Institute Success, accessed May 13, 2024, https://institutesuccess.com/library/the-first-step-towards-getting-somewhere-is-to-decide-youre-not-going-to-stay-where-you-are-john-pierpont-morgan-2/.

49 Sadock, Sadock, and Ruiz, Synopsis of Psychiatry, 8-9.

50 Harold A. Sackeim et al., "Clinical Outcomes in a Large Registry of Patients with Major Depressive Disorder Treated with Transcranial Magnetic Stimulation," Journal of Affective Disorders 277, (December 2020): 65-74, https://doi.org/10.1016/j.jad.2020.08.005.

51 "BrainyQuote," "Brian Tracy - You cannot control what happens to you, but...", BrainyQuote, accessed June 4, 2024, https://www.brainyquote.com/quotes/brian_tracy_125679.

52 Maltz, Psycho-Cybernetics, 212.

53 Maltz, Psycho-Cybernetics, 121.

54 Shannon Kaiser, The Self-Love Experiment: Fifteen Principles for Becoming More Kind, Compassionate, and Accepting of Yourself (New York: TarcherPerigee, 2017), 139.

55 Maltz, Psycho-Cybernetics, 148.

56 Maltz, Psycho-Cybernetics, 62.

57 Wayne Dyer, The Power of Intention (New York: Hay House, 2006), 43.

58 Walter D. Wintle, "Thinking by Walter D Wintle," All Poetry, accessed May 13, 2024, https://allpoetry.com/poem/8624439-Thinking-by-Walter-D-Wintle.

59 Maltz, Psycho-Cybernetics, 121; Ampere A. Tseng, "Scientific Evidence of Health Benefits by Practicing Mantra Meditation: Narrative Review," International Journal of Yoga 15, no. 2 (May-Aug 2022): 89-95, https://doi.org/10.4103/ijoy.ijoy_53_22.

60 Maltz, Psycho-Cybernetics, 56, 118.

61 Maltz, Psycho-Cybernetics, 84.

62 Maltz, Psycho-Cybernetics, 121.

63   Maltz, Psycho-Cybernetics, 220.

64   Maltz, Psycho-Cybernetics, 45.

65   "Optimism," Psychology Today Canada, accessed June 4, 2024, https://
     www.psychologytoday.com/ca/basics/optimism.

66   Maltz, Psycho-Cybernetics, 157-159.

67   Sadock, Sadock, and Ruiz, Synopsis of Psychiatry, 186.

68   Charlotte Sidebotham, "Good Enough is Good Enough!" British Journal
     of General Practice 67, no. 660 (July 2017): 311, https://doi.org/10.3399/
     bjgp17X691409; Sadock, Sadock, and Ruiz, Synopsis of Psychiatry, 1093.

69   Maltz, Psycho-Cybernetics, 148.

70   Trafton, Gordon, and Misra, Training Your Brain to Adopt Healthful
     Habits, 44; Winston and Seif, Overcoming Unwanted Intrusive
     Thoughts, 140.

71   Trafton, Gordon, and Misra, Training Your Brain to Adopt Healthful
     Habits, 250.

72   Sutton, "Martin Seligman's Positive Psychology Theory."

73   Maltz, Psycho-Cybernetics, 115.

74   Waldinger, "Author Talks."

75   Carol Mattson Porth, Essentials of Pathophysiology: Concepts of
     Altered States, 4th ed. (Philadelphia: Wolters Kluwer, 2015), 208.

76   Waldinger, "Author Talks."

77   Waldinger, "Author Talks."

78   "It's a Funny Thing about Life, Once You Begin to Take Note of the Things
     You Are Grateful For, You Begin to Lose Sight of the Things That You Lack,"
     Quotespedia, accessed May 13, 2024, https://www.quotespedia.org/

authors/g/germany-kent/its-a-funny-thing-about-life-once-you-begin-to-take-note-of-the-things-you-are-grateful-for-you-begin-to-lose-sight-of-the-things-that-you-lack-germany-kent/.

79 A. Pascual-Leone et al. "Modulation of Muscle Responses Evoked by Transcranial Magnetic Stimulation During the Acquisition of New Fine Motor Skills," Journal of Neurophysiology 74, no. 3 (September 1995): 1037, https://doi.org/10.1152/jn.1995.74.3.1037.

80 Maltz, Psycho-Cybernetics, 43.

81 Maltz, Psycho-Cybernetics, xxi-xxii.

82 Maltz, Psycho-Cybernetics, 43.

83 David Hamilton, "Can You Use Your Mind to Improve Your Strength?" DrDavidHamilton.com, August 11, 2022, https://drdavidhamilton.com/can-you-use-your-mind-to-improve-your-strength/; Ranganathan et al. "From Mental Power to Muscle Power—Gaining Strength By Using the Mind," Neuropsychologia 42, no. 7 (2004): 944-56, https://doi.org/10.1016/j.neuropsychologia.2003.11.018.

84 Fuu-Jiun Hwang et al. "Motor Learning Selectively Strengthens Cortical and Striatal Synapses of Motor Engram Neurons," Neuron 110, no. 17, (September 7): 2790-801, https://doi.org/10.1016/j.neuron.2022.06.006.

85 David R. Hamilton, How Your Mind Can Heal Your Body (New York: Hay House, 2010).

86 David Hamilton, "Visualization Alters the Brain and Body," DrDavidHamilton, April 19, 2011, https://drdavidhamilton.com/visualisation-alters-the-brain-body/.

87 Hamilton, "Can You Use Your Mind to Improve Your Strength?"

88 Sadock, Sadock, and Ruiz, Synopsis of Psychiatry, 110.

89 Maltz, Psycho-Cybernetics, 28.

90 Maltz, Psycho-Cybernetics, 263-4.

91 Maltz, Psycho-Cybernetics, 263.

92 Maltz, Psycho-Cybernetics, 263.

93 "The Secret of Change Is to Focus All of Your Energy, Not on Fighting the Old, But on Building the New," Quote Investigator, May 28, 2013, https://quoteinvestigator.com/2013/05/28/socrates-energy/.

94 "Action this Day!" International Churchill Society, August 19, 2021, https://winstonchurchill.org/the-life-of-churchill/life/man-of-action/action-this-day-27/.

95 Maltz, Psycho-Cybernetics, 148.

96 Maltz, Psycho-Cybernetics, 149.

97 Maltz, Psycho-Cybernetics, 129.

98 Maltz, Psycho-Cybernetics, 2.

99 Irvin D. Yalom, Theory and Practice of Group Psychotherapy, 5th ed. (New York: Perseus Books, 2005); Leslie M. Lothstein and Kathryn Thomas, "The Theory and Practice of Group Psychotherapy, Sixth Edition," review of The Theory and Practice of Group Psychotherapy, by Irvin D. Yalom and Molyn Leszcz, The American Journal of Psychotherapy 74, no. 2 (June 2021): 98-9, https://doi.org/10.1176/appi.psychotherapy.20210007.

100 "Everything Has Beauty, but not Everyone Sees it." BrainyQuote, accessed May 13, 2024, https://www.brainyquote.com/quotes/confucius_104254.

101 "Resolve to Be Tender with the Young and Compassionate with the Aged," Quote Investigator, December 22, 2014, https://quoteinvestigator.com/2014/12/22/tender/#:~:text=Most%20of%20the%20page%20was,have%20been%20all%20of%20these.%E2%80%9D.

102 Elizabeth Dori Tunstall, "How Maya Angelou Made Me Feel," The Conversation, May 29, 2014, https://theconversation.com/how-maya-angelou-made-me-feel-27328.

103 Murshid Akram, "Gandhi Quotes About Animals," September 19, 2021, https://peoplesquotes.com/gandhi-quotes-about-animals.

104 Clare Pooley, The Authenticity Project (New York: Pamela Dorman Books, 2020), 173.

105 Floriana NK, One Day or Day One. You Decide (self-pub, 2021).

106 Waldinger, "Author Talks."

107 "Folks Are Usually about as Happy as They Make Up Their Minds to Be."

108 "Sometimes People Complicate Things by Thinking Too Much About What Someone Might Think of What They Said or Did," BrainyQuote, accessed May 13, 2024, https://www.brainyquote.com/quotes/derek_jeter_668784.

109 "Your Image Isn't Your Character. Character Is What You Are as a Person," BrainyQuote, accessed May 13, 2024, https://www.brainyquote.com/quotes/derek_jeter_586278#:~:text=Derek%20Jeter%20Quotes&text=Please%20enable%20Javascript-,Your%20image%20isn't%20your%20character.,you%20are%20as%20a%20person.

110 "Tools Quotes," AZ Quotes, accessed May 13, 2024, https://www.azquotes.com/quotes/topics/tools.html#google_vignette.

111 Maltz, Psycho-Cybernetics, 147.

112 "Whatever the Mind of Man Can Conceive and Believe, it can Achieve," BrainyQuote, May 13, 2024, https://www.brainyquote.com/quotes/napoleon_hill_39225.

Made in the USA
Las Vegas, NV
08 December 2024

13590920R10085